CISTERCIAN STUDIES NUMI

André Vauchez

THE SPIRITUALITY OF
THE MEDIEVAL WEST

From the Eighth to the Twelfth Century

CISTERCIAN STUDIES NUMBER ONE HUNDRED FORTY-FIVE

THE SPIRITUALITY OF THE MEDIEVAL WEST

From the Eighth to the Twelfth Century

by
André Vauchez

Translated from the French by
Colette Friedlander

Cistercian Publications
Kalamazoo, Michigan

A translation of *La spiritualité de
moyen-âge occidental VIII-XII siècles*,
published by Les Presses Universitaires de la France, 1975

Cistercian Publications

Editorial Offices
The Institute of Cistercian Studies
Western Michigan University
Kalamazoo, Michigan 49008-5415
cistpub@wmich.edu

*The work of Cistercian Publications is made possible in part by support from Western
Michigan University to The Institute of Cistercian Studies.*

Printed in the United States of America

TABLE OF CONTENTS

INTRODUCTION

SPIRITUALITY: what is the meaning of this term? In beginning the present book, we must define the notion as precisely as possible, for it has been understood very differently by various periods and authors. It was unknown in the Middle Ages, which merely distinguished between *doctrina*, that is, the dogmatic and normative aspect of faith, and *disciplina*, its implementation, generally within the framework of a religious rule. The word *spiritualitas*, sometimes found in philosophical texts from the twelfth century onward, has no specifically religious content: it refers to the quality of that which is spiritual, that is, independent of matter. Spirituality is, in fact, a modern concept, in use only since the nineteenth century. As understood by most authors, it expresses the religious dimension of the inner life and implies an art of asceticism, leading through mysticism to the establishment of a personal relationship with God. When this experience, after being systematically formulated, is passed on by a master to his disciples by means of teaching or of written texts, we speak of spiritual movements or of schools of spirituality. Thus we traditionally single out a franciscan spirituality, an ignatian spirituality, and so on.

We have chosen not to content ourselves with this definition, which has little significance for periods earlier than the thirteenth century. Had we done so, we would have had to limit our study to what was numerically a very small group, coinciding roughtly with an elite—the religious. For between the eighth and twelfth centuries, only in the peace of the cloister—at least of some cloisters, for all were not sanctuaries of meditation and recollection—could an intense spiritual life develop, one centered on the quest for contemplation and expressed in ascetical treatises or biblical commentaries. But the history of spirituality cannot be restricted to an inventory and an analysis of the works which register the inner experience of monks. Next to the explicit spirituality of clerics and religious formulated in writing, there is, in our opinion, another; it has left few traces in texts, but its reality emerges thanks to such other means of expression as gesture, song, and iconography. In this perspective, spirituality is no longer viewed as a system codifying rules for the inner life, but as a relationship between, on one hand, aspects of the christian mystery which were particularly highlighted during a given period and, on the other, practices—such as rituals, prayers and devotions—which were themselves privileged with regard to other practices possible within the christian life. Scripture indeed conveys so many different elements that every civilization is led to make choices according to its cultural level and its specific needs. These variations doubtless remain within bounds set by the basic principles of revelation and tradition, bounds which may not be transgressed without lapsing into heresy. But during the Middle Ages—a period when dogmatic cohesion was not yet well ensured in all areas and when there was a deep gulf between the literate elite and the uneducated masses—there was room even within orthodoxy for different ways of interpreting and living the christian message, that is, for different spiritualities. Our purpose will be to retrace the history of their formation, of their sometimes difficult coexistence, and of their succession in time. The demands of an historical presentation of these religious phenomena will inevitably lead us to emphasize changes. We must take care not to forget that the appearance of a new spirituality only rarely brought about the disappearance of the one that had formerly prevailed: the rise of Cîteaux did not prevent Cluny from continuing on its own way. It simply relegated it to a position of secondary importance.

This definition of spirituality as the dynamic unity between the content of a faith and the way in which it is lived by historically determined human beings, will lead us to devote a good deal of space to the laity. Not that we intend to honor a trend, or to minimize *a priori* the role and influence of the clergy. But since, until recently, attention has been focused too exclusively on the latter, bringing out the originality of popular spirituality seems to be in keeping with fairness and historical objectivity. Although such a concept is not devoid of ambiguity and is still an object of controversy among specialists,[1] it nevertheless remains valid at a very general level. We will indeed come to see in the course of this book, as other historians have for other periods, that persons of 'low estate' integrated into their personal and collective religious experience various elements, some derived from the religion they had been taught, others provided by the mentality common to their environment and their time and marked by representations and beliefs foreign to Christianity. As they were, moreover, unable to attain to abstraction, lay people had a tendency to transpose the basic mysteries of faith onto an emotional register. Are we therefore to conclude that popular religion is no more than an incoherent set of practices and devotions? We do not think so. The illiterate, who made up the immense majority of the faithful between the eighth and twelfth centuries, had a notion of God and of man's relation to the divine which certainly deserves to be called spirituality. Thus, rather than doctrines and schools of spirituality, which have already been the object of intensive study,[2] our focus

[1]See the first findings of an investigation on 'popular spirituality' in *Revue d'Histoire de la Spiritualité* 49 (1973) 493-504.

[2]Particularly in the basic work by Jean Leclercq, François Vandenbroucke and Louis Bouyer, *La spiritualité du Moyen Age* (Paris, 1961). ET: *The Spirituality of the Middle Ages* (London, 1963).

will be the christian message's possible impact on the mind and behavior of the greater number. In other words, we will attempt to bring the history of spirituality down from the summits where it has too often been pleased to dwell, and to place it within the social and cultural history of the medieval West.

I

THE GENESIS OF MEDIEVAL SPIRITUALITY

From the Eighth to the Early Tenth Century

WHEN ANTIQUITY ends and the Middle Ages begin is very difficult to determine, even more with regard to the spiritual life than in the field of political or economic history. A number of facts lead us to think that the transition from one type of religiosity to another occurred rather late. Christianity's cultural heritage was, at least at first, taken over for the most part by the barbarian kingdoms which grew up on the ruins of the Roman Empire; sometimes they even enriched it, as can be seen in visigothic Spain. On the other hand, the rise of monasticism, often regarded as a specifically medieval phenomenon, actually carried on fourth-century ascetic currents, a living synthesis of which Saint Martin, in Gaul, had achieved. It is, in fact, quite normal that continuity should long have prevailed over change in the history of a religion which viewed its original period as a necessary reference and an ideal norm.

Other reasons have also led us to set the starting point for the present study of medieval spirituality as late as the early eighth century. There can be no talk of spiritual life until there has first been, not only formal adhesion to a body of doctrine, but also some permeation of both individuals and societies by the religious beliefs they profess; and this can take place only over time. But in most of the western countryside—apart from the mediterranenan area—the population was not

11

completely converted to the christian faith until the 700s. The date was later still in some areas of Germany, where paganism survived until the time of Charlemagne. All in all, only in the eighth century did Christianity fully become the religion of the West. During that century, the West experienced its first attempts at building a christian society. Invested with supernatural power by virtue of their coronation, the carolingian monarchs considered themselves responsible for the salvation of their people and claimed to rule the Church just as they did secular society. Charlemagne, who pushed these principles to their ultimate consequences, appeared to his contemporaries as a 'new Constantine', a restorer of the christian empire. But in this, as in other areas, the authors of the carolingian renaissance, while striving to return to tradition, could not avoid innovating considerably, so different had the world they lived in become. Their action, which aimed at restoring the christian religion to its ancient splendor, in the end resulted in the triumph of a spirituality far removed from that of the Fathers of the Church. One of these features we will now study.

<h3 style="text-align:center">RETURN TO THE OLD TESTAMENT</h3>

At every stage in the life of the Church, Christians have made choices within the vast biblical heritage and have shown a special preference for some episodes or figures which met their aspirations better than others. The high Middle Ages was especially attracted to the Old Testament, more attuned than the New to the state of the society and mentality of the time. It is certainly not by chance that in one of the rare mosaics of the period which have come down to us— that of Germigny-des-Prés—God is portrayed as the Ark of the Covenant. In the superficially christianized West, which a centralizing governement was attempting to unify with the support of the clergy, the Jerusalem of kings and high priests was bound to exercise a special fascination. Moreover, the

Church of the time seems to have been concerned mainly with incarnation and establishment, with seeking to build the City of God on earth. In the pursuit of this goal, it met with support from secular authority: the monarchs gave force of law to ecclesiastical decrees which, during the previous period, had often gone unheeded for lack of a secular arm to implement them. In 755, for instance, Pippin reiterated in a capitulary the decisions of the Council of Ver regarding Sunday obligation and abstention from work that day. The same occurred regarding the payment of tithes to the clergy, which the Carolingians rendered compulsory. In return, the Church prayed for the king, provided him with a portion of his officials, and contributed to ensuring his subjects' loyalty by conferring a sacred quality on oaths, which, beginning with Charlemagne, became the foundation of the political system.

Historians have often remembered only the more spectacular aspects of this similarity between high medieval christendom and the Israel of old: Charlemagne's being called 'David' or 'new Josiah', or the anointing which, conferred by the hands of bishops on the kings of the West—Wamba in Toledo in 672, Pippin in 751, Egfrid in England in 787—made them the successors of Saul and Solomon. But the Old Testament's influence left a far deeper mark on religious mentalities and on spiritual life.[1] It was during the carolingian period that Christianity became a matter of outward practices and obedience to rules. To repeat Saint Paul's terms, the Gospel had freed man from slavery to the Law, but this ideal of spiritual freedom was beyond the reach of the barbarian peoples whose settlement on the ruins of the Roman Empire was, in Focillon's words, 'prehistory bursting into history'. Through contact with them, and as it penetrated deeply into the countryside, the christian faith ran the risk of deteriorating into a set of superstitious practices. In this

[1]Yves Congar, 'Deux facteurs de sacralisation de la vie sociale au Moyen Age (en Occident)', *Concilium* 47 (1969) 53–63.

perspective, compelling the baptized to live once more under the Law by restoring Old Testament observances can, paradoxically, appear as spiritual progress.

In actual fact, the process had begun two centuries earlier within celtic christendom, where the Church had advocated literal imitation of Old Testament institutions and legal provisions, imposing respectful submission of the faithful to the clergy and obedience of the clergy to its hierarchical superiors. Under the influence of 'scottish' monks, many judaizing practices had subsequently penetrated onto the continent, for instance, the equating of Sunday with the Sabbath and the legal obligation of tithes. The impact of the old Law was especially strong in the field of sexual morality, where many levitic precepts were re-enforced: women were regarded as unclean after chilbirth and were excluded from church until the ceremony of churching, abstention from sexual relations was required during certain periods of the liturgical year, severe penances were inflicted for nocturnal pollution, and so on. Most of these prohibitions and penalties remained in force until the thirteenth century. That bespeaks how deep a mark they left on the moral consciousness of medieval man.

During the carolingian period, religious practice was less an expression of inner adhesion than a social obligation. While some clerics reasserted the traditional doctrine regarding the freedom of the act of faith (as did Alcuin at the time of the forced christianization of the Saxons), laymen—first and foremost Charlemagne—had no qualms whatever about putting the maxim 'Force them to enter' *(Compelle intrare)* into practice with the utmost brutality. The idea emerged that all the christian emperor's subjects—except for the Jews, a small group—must worship the same God as he, simply because they were under his authority. Not only did this administrative view of religion justify forced conversions, it legitimated the use of physical constraint by secular rulers for the purpose of suppressing schisms and heresies. Faith was considered first of all as a trust which it was the monarch's responsibility to preserve and pass on in its entirety. Thus we see Charlemagne convene and preside over councils charged with deciding such points of doctrine as the procession of the Holy Spirit and the veneration of images, or, in the *General admonition* (*Admonitio generalis*) of 789, multiplying rules and exhortations regarding the religious life of clerics and lay people. In such a spiritual climate, which equated the Church with the biblical 'people of God', the very notion of the priesthood was strongly influenced by the mosaic model of worship. Carolingian priests were men of prayer and sacrifice rather than preachers or witnesses; they were closely related to the Levites. In the eyes of the faithful they were specialists of the sacred, set apart by their knowledge of the effective rituals and formulas. The very evolution of the sacrament of orders is expressive of this tendency to single out the clergy. Formerly conferred simply by the laying on of hands, it henceforth included an anointing which made the priest the Lord's anointed one, according to the ritual described in the Book of Numbers (Nb 3:3). The Carolingians favored the clergy's propensity to form a priestly caste, separated from the rest of the people by its duties and status. By instituting episcopal monarchy—one resident bishop in every diocese, one metropolitan archbishop in every province—and a territorial church—that is, the obligation enjoined on the faithful to practice their religion within the framework of their own parish—, they contributed to the greater cohesion of that body. This clergy, settled and organized into a hierarchy, was moreover endowed with legal privileges. Were not churches themselves sacred spaces, so that those who took refuge in them benefited from a right of asylum acknowledged by civil law since the seventh century? As for the clerics who ministered to them, they enjoyed the privilege of forum, which removed them and their property from lay jurisdiction, as well as tithes which provided for their support and for that of the poor.

A LITURGICAL CIVILIZATION

Such an evolution can be better understood by considering the importance taken on by worship within Christianity during the high Middle Ages. The carolingian period has been called a 'liturgical civilization'.[2] The expression is a correct one if it is taken to mean that religion was then identified with the worship rendered to God by the priests who were its ministers. The faithful were under a moral and legal obligation to attend it. Not even monasticism escaped this atmosphere: under the influence of Benedict of Aniane the liturgy took on growing prominence in the monks' life, to the detriment of the apostolic activities which had been so important in the days of Saint Columban and Saint Boniface.

That being said, we must examine the spirit of this liturgy. Outside the monasteries, it does seem that it ceased to be the community expression of a people in prayer, and became, in the eyes of the faithful, a set of rituals from which they hoped to profit. Ritualism was, in fact, one of the outstanding features of religious life at the time. The emperor set an example by insisting, in various capitularies, that the priests have correct liturgical texts at their disposal and by earnestly recommending that they see to the cleanliness of the sacred vessels. In his eyes, the scrupulous observance of ritual was essential if divine worship was to exert all its saving effects, from which both individuals and the entire community benefited. Here again, Old Testament influence made a forceful comeback: eighth-century sacramentaries were enriched with new celebrations which drew their inspiration directly from the Book of Exodus, such as those accompanying the dedication of churches—a sumptuous ritual characterized by much sprinkling of holy water and incensing—or the royal coronation.

In the Mass itself, the ecclesial dimension of the sacrifice took second place. Individualism was, for that matter, one of the basic components of the religious climate of the time: this may be seen in the case of priests who began to celebrate private, unattended Masses and votive Masses for particular intentions.

[2]E. Delaruelle, 'La Gaule chrétienne à l'époque franque,' *Revue d'Histoire de l'Eglise de France* 38 (1952) 64–72.

As for lay people, they no longer played an active part in worship, which had become the prerogative of specialists. Liturgical singing, in fact, took up more and more of the services; difficult as it was, it could be performed only by cantors trained in cathedral schools or monasteries. In many areas, the adoption of gregorian—or roman—chant under Charlemagne's influence introduced modes of expression foreign to the local liturgy, thereby making the participation of the faithful even more difficult. The later evolution of religious chant was, moreover, to be in the direction of growing complexity, with the appearance in the tenth century of polyphony (at first in two parts), particularly in the abbeys of Sankt Gallen and Saint-Amand. The internal layout of churches could only favor passivity on the part of the faithful: they stood in the nave, separated from the sanctuary by the chancel and from the altar by choirs of clerics chanting in the *schola cantorum*. The celebrant stood with his back to them and addressed God in their name. From the eighth century onward, the priest, who had until then offered the eucharistic sacrifice with the words: 'They who offer you this sacrifice of praise' (*qui tibi offerunt hoc sacrificium laudis*) felt compelled to add: 'or for whom we offer it to you' (*vel pro quibus tibi offerimus*). This aptly conveys the rift that had opened between clergy and faithful. 'Physically present at a sometimes brilliant, most often drab performance, whose meaning was on the whole unknown to them, unused to praying privately, rarely called upon to pray in common, lay people were bored at Mass for lack of participation.'[3]

The fact that Latin remained the liturgical language also contributed to rendering liturgy foreign to the faithful. It may appear surprising that, even in areas where virtually the entire population spoke only germanic idioms, the use of the vernacular did not succeed in gaining acceptance in the field

[3]J. Chelini, 'La pratique dominicale dans l'Eglise franque', *Revue d'Histoire de l'Eglise de France* 42 (1956) 161–174.

of worship, as it did at the same time in the slavic lands christianized by Byzantium. But as the sole written language, and thus the only one that could be used in the liturgy, Latin enjoyed unrivaled prestige. Moreover, carolingian clerics were fascinated by Rome and its culture, and all their efforts in the field of literature were aimed at restoring good latinity and the use of classical forms. Translating the Vulgate into the romanic or germanic tongue would have seemed to them both a sacrilegious and a useless undertaking, since in any case very lay persons knew how to read. As a result, command of the language of worship became the exclusive privilege of clerics, and the liturgy turned into a new discipline of the secret.

More serious yet—and fraught with consequences—was the new notion of eucharistic sacrifice which began to prevail at the time. As has been aptly shown by J. A. Jungmann,[4] the carolingian Mass was less a thanksgiving on the part of the faithful than a gift to men from God descending from heaven to earth. This coming took place during the canon, henceforth recited in a low voice as if to underline the mysterious aspect of the transformation of the bread and wine. Moreover, the development of the rites contributed to making Christians lose sight of the relation between the sacrament and daily life. From the eighth century onward, leavened bread was no longer used for communion; it was replaced by round, white, unleavened hosts, and the consecrated wine was distributed to the faithful only on very rare occasions. There was no longer any breaking of bread, and the assembly's offerings were reduced to a few coins. The faithful, henceforth kneeling at the communion rail, received the sacrament in their mouths and no longer in their hands. This concern with eliminating everything realistic and concrete from the sacrament of the altar was given yet more emphasis by some great carolingian prelates. Amalarius of Metz in particular, author of an important liturgical treatise entitled *Church Services* (*De ecclesiasticis*

---

[4] J. A. Jungmann, *Missarum solemnia* (Paris: 1964) 1:106–126.

officiis), gave a symbolic interpretation of the Mass: according to him, the succeeding phases of the ceremony, the celebrant's vestments, and the liturgical objects referred, by virtue of subtle analogies, to various biblical episodes. In this perspective, the Holy Sacrifice in its entirety became a sort of allegory commemorating the life of Jesus. Although Amalarius' ideas were condemned by the synod of Quierzy in 838, they finally gained recognition and prevailed throughout most of the Middle Ages.

During eucharistic celebrations, the reception of Christ's body seems to have been infrequent. In the eighth century, Saint Boniface recommended it on great occasions, that is, on the main feasts of the liturgical cycle: Christmas, Easter and Pentecost. At the same time, however, he warned the faithful against sacrilegious communions. The latter bit of advice seems to have been heeded more than the former. When Ambrose Autpert spelled out the duties of lay people, he spoke of fasting, mortifications, and alms, but did not mention communion. When it did, however, take place, it seemed to occasion a contact with the divine which appeared magical rather than spiritual : communion, for the faithful, primarily meant taking out a security on the mysterious and terrible deity in whose name the saints performed great miracles. As late as the eleventh century, peasants are known to have taken consecrated hosts and buried pieces of them in the ground in order to increase its fertility. Such practices, and other similar ones mentioned in the penitentials of the time, doubtless explain the clerics' reservations and their lack of eagerness to give their flocks communion.

CAROLINGIAN MORALISM

To reduce all of the religiosity of carolingian times to pure ritualism would, however, give a distorted view of it. The thinly interiorized faith of the era sought expression in other registers, and especially realization in works. E. Delaruelle has stressed the positive value of this 'carolingian moralism' which tended to awaken individuals to the ethical demands of Christianity: in particular, it reintroduced the notions of justice and virtue into the political arena by way of the imperial ideology.[5] The merovingian king was, in effect, a despot who derived his power from blood descent. His high-handedness was limited only by civil war, assassination, and superstitious fear of God and his saints. The carolingian monarch, on account of his role in the Church and in society, appeared as a true shepherd entrusted with the care of souls. This new concept of the royal office was a consequence of the coronation rite. It endowed the ruler with supernatural prestige, but the bishops, who anointed him, henceforth had a hold over him. 'Sacred' kingship was not far removed from the ministerial concept of secular power, according to which the monarch's mission consisted in putting the structures of the state at the Church's service. The last visigothic kings had had a bitter taste of this on the eve of the arab conquest. The same phenomenon repeated itself in the carolingian empire as early as the reign of Louis the Pious, who, under pressure from both bishops and lords, was compelled to perform public penance at Saint-Médard at Soissons in 833 for having been remiss in his duties towards his sons. For the ruler was judged primarily on his conduct, which had to be a model for his subjects. The Church could withdraw its support from the king if it deemed that he had become unworthy. The weaker the authority of the carolingian monarchs became, the more they were reminded of their duties by such prelates as Hincmar, archbishop of Reims, who showed himself especially demanding in this respect.

What was true for the king was also true for the princes and lords surrounding him. In the ninth century, clerics wrote *Mirrors for Princes* (*Specula principis*) aimed at this upper aristocracy. A good deal of space was devoted to moral

[5]E. Delaruelle, 'Jonas d'Orleans et le moralisme carolingien', *Bulletin de Littérature ecclésiastique* 55 (1954) 129–143.

demands. The emphasis lay especially on the importance of carrying out the duties of one's state: the powerful (*potentes*) were invited to put their power at the service of the christian ideal and to use it in favor of the Church and of the weak. That these writings seem to have had some influence, at least in the circles for which they were intended, is evidenced by treatises on the spiritual life, or for purposes of edification, written by aristocrats themselves. One such work was the *Manual* authored about 843 by Dhuoda, wife of Bernard, marquess of Septimania, for the benefit of her eldest son. The pious lady presented the christian life as a struggle involving constant effort: after long and perilous contests against the vices, the soul climbs the fifteen steps of perfection and overcomes evil by penance, prayer, and almsgiving. This last was a strict obligation for the powerful; in return, it ensured them the gratitude of the poor whose duty it was to pray to God for their benefactors.

Such treatises could not, however, raise the religious level of society as a whole. The great majority of lay persons were quite indifferent to this literature, which did no more than plagiarize the codes of spiritual life drawn up for clerics. The fact was grasped by one of the best minds of the time, Bishop Jonas of Orleans, author of an essay entitled *The Education of the Laity* (*De institutione laicali*, ca. 830). In it he attempted to offer the faithful—and especially husbands and wives— teaching suited to their state. It contains interesting developments on the sanctification of marriage and on conjugal morality, as well as on the pastoral ministry proper to heads of families. But the treatise's originality lies less in its content than in its aims. Jonas of Orleans was attempting to lay the basis for an *ordo laicorum*, that is, a form of christian life for the faithful comparable to that which the Church and civil authority were trying to induce the clergy to adopt. Indeed, since the end of the eighth century clerics had been called upon to become a canonical body (*ordo canonicus*) by following the rule of Saint Chrodegang (d.766). The latter obligated clerics to the practice of the common life; it implied regular attendance at the divine office and continence. Similarly, the Carolingians had striven to reform monasticism by imposing stability on religious and by introducing uniform observance within a monastic body (*ordo monasticus*) governed by the rule of Saint Benedict. The idea of extending the benefit of a regulated, if not regular, lifestyle to the laity was an original one, but doubtless too daring for the times. Although the Church did succeed in having the authorities forbid divorce and incest, it failed in its efforts to moralize the sexual life of the layfolk and was unable to put an end to abductions and common law marriages. On the whole, however, the spiritual effects of carolingian moralism were positive to the extent that it brought out the ethical demands of the christian faith and the need to give them expression in behavior.

The same basic concern inspired changes in the sacrament of penance. Beginning in the seventh century, irish and 'scottish' monks had spread the system of fixed-rate penance on the continent—a system which broke with the discipline of ancient times. During the first centuries of Christianity the penitential process had been a public, community affair: the penitent had had to present himself before the bishop at the beginning of Lent in order to be reconciled by him before the church assembly on Holy Thursday, at the close of solemn and complex ceremonies. Moreover, since he could have access to penance only once in his lifetime, the sinner remained subject until his death to numerous prohibitions; these cut him off in particular from marital and social life. Conversely, according to the new discipline, the sacrament could be repeated as often as the faithful judged necessary. All they had to do was to approach an ordinary priest, or even, in case of necessity, a lay person. The sin was remitted once the penalties inflicted by the confessor had been carried out; they were determined according to a rate indicated in books called penitentials. The entire process remained secret and purely private; the Church intervened only in the person of the priest. These new customs were especially suited to minds long familiar with the idea of a compensation—the *wergeld* or compensatory fine—whose amount was set by a court as amends for bloodshed. The church hierarchy attempted to oppose this transformation of the sacrament and to restore the rules of ancient times in all their strictness; all it succeeded in achieving, during the carolingian period, was dissociating cases of public misdeeds, for which public penance was required, from secret ones, for which private penance according to the fixed-rate system was acceptable.[6]

The success the new forms met with is easy to explain: the faithful, who led bad lives and prayed little, felt crushed by a feeling of guilt from which they could hope to be freed only at the hour of death. They joyfully welcomed the possibility of obtaining absolution as often as they wished through confession and atonement for their misdeeds. All the same, the penalties provided by the penitentials were very heavy; they had been determined by the celtic monks for a still-pagan people upon whom they dreamed of imposing an ascetic ideal. Hence some punishments included an impressive number of months—if not years—of fasts and various other mortifications. In spite of the refining which these texts underwent in carolingian times—evidenced, for instance, by the penitential of Halitgarius, bishop of Cambrai—, the penalties remained stringent, often too stringent for a single person. This led to the practice—encountered very frequently as early as the eighth century—of redeeming canonical penances by substituting deeds which were easier to perform, and even, by the end of the ninth century, fines or donations in money; this was accepted for the first time in 895, at the synod of Tribur. Restricted at first to certain misdeeds, the practice was soon extended to all of them. This was a significant development in that it implied constant pressure on the clergy from the laity for the purpose of obtaining the remission of their sins on better terms.

[6]C. Vogel, *Le pécheur et la penitence au Moyen Age* (Paris: 1966) especially p. 15 to 27.

Highly materialistic as these practices were, the effect of the new penitential discipline was an enhancement of the religious level of the faithful. The penitentials spread throughout the West a classification of sins which allowed for a refining of the moral life; next after the three irremissible sins of the early Church—idolatry, fornication and manslaughter—, the eight capital sins appeared there for the first time: gluttony, lust, greed, anger, dejection, *acedia* (pessimism, world-weariness), conceit, pride. Moreover, they expressed a very simple notion of penance, one based on the old medical precept of healing by opposites (*contraria contrariis sanantur*). Thus, to obtain forgiveness, the greedy cleric would have to give generous alms, the unstable one lead a sedentary life. Was the sacrament's foremost objective not the restoration of an inner balance upset by sin? Devoid of spiritual ambition, these texts conveyed a very practical and concrete notion of humanity's relation to God, seen as guarantor of the moral law. The absolution of sin depended on human efforts and on human zeal in atoning for the misdeed one has committed, but deed was presented primarily as an offence to God, whose forgiveness was conditional on a request and a feeling of contrition. Thus, by means of fixed-rate penance, a new type of relationship began to emerge 'between the Christian and a God who dispensed his graces in exchange for sacrifices'.[7]

POPULAR RELIGIOSITY AND CHRISTIAN SPIRITUALITY

In the last analysis, such changes in penitential discipline expressed the faithful's yearning for a way of access to salvation despite the handicap their state entailed in that regard. Indeed, because of the cleavages which had developed within the Church, the sacred had become the prerogative of clerics and monks, who alone had the possibility of devoting themselves to prayer, the recitation of psalms, and the reading of

[7]G. Le Bras, 'Les pénitentiels irlandais', in *Le miracle irlandais* (Paris: 1956) p.172–207.

Scripture. Within the upper aristocracy, an elite of literate lay people no doubt imitated this type of religious life, as is shown by the existence of *Libelli precum*, prayer booklets intended for the faithful and closely inspired by liturgical prayer. But the masses did not have access to such texts, and were content with the few religious practices which punctuated their unreligious lives: abstinence from marital relations at set times, fasting during Lent, attendance at Sunday Mass, and the payment of tithes. Quite understandably, the hunger for the divine which may have lurked in them was not satisfied by a program so limited in its outlook. Thus they were tempted to look elsewhere for an answer to their quest.

Here we encounter the very delicate question of popular religion. Through indirect evidence, particularly condemnations formulated by councils or contained in penitentials, we can perceive that the spiritual life of the masses extended beyond the constraining framework of the ecclesiastical institution, if not of christian dogma. This is true not only of areas freshly torn away from paganism, such as Saxony, for which a *List of Superstitions* (*Indiculus superstitionum*), drawn up soon after the land had been conquered by Charlemagne, provides us with a fairly precise list of local beliefs. Even in areas which had been christianized longer, the official religion was still, in many cases, no more than a veneer superficially masking heterogenous elements labeled 'superstitions' by the clerics. Not that ancient or germanic paganism had survived as a consistent body of doctrines—something it had never been in any case. But a whole network of institutions and practices, some of them doubtless very old, made up the warp of a religious life which unfolded on the fringes of christian worship. We cannot, for instance, determine the exact activities of the lay 'guilds' and 'confraternities' denounced by Archbishop Hincmar of Reims, but we may legitimately suppose that mutual aid was not their only function. The importance given the stars and any extraordinary occurrences in the sky can more easily be grasped.[8] As Bishop Burchard of Worms noted as late as the threshold of the eleventh century in his penitential entitled *Corrector or Physician* (*Corrector sive medicus*), the faithful worshiped the elements, the course of the stars and even eclipses. The new moon was a crucial moment which people awaited before building houses or contracting marriages. At that time of the month nocturnal gatherings were held, during which, according to the prelate, 'they try to restore the new moon to its brilliance by cries or otherwise; they let out howls to come to the help of the stars or to await help from them'.[9] In another passage of his treatise, he puts the following question to his penitent: 'Did you pray elsewhere than in church, that is, near a spring, near stones, near trees, or at a crossroads?'[10] Other penitentials punished reliance on amulets and spells, as well as belief in witches, enchanters, and evil spirits.

Such descriptions, imprecise as they are, compel us to ask what sort of notion most of Charlemagne's or Hincmar's contemporaries had of God: he was doubtless perceived as a mysterious force which could reveal itself at any time or place. But this power was believed to be especially present in holy places, and was not thought to exercise itself blindly. In the general mentality, it was more or less confusedly identified with good and right; it guaranteed oaths and punished perjurers. In some circumstances, it could not fail to intervene in favor of the innocent and to point out the guilty. This was the religious foundation of ordeals, chief among them trial by fire or by water and judicial duelling. This last was the ordinary means of proof in the case of free men. In 809, Charlemagne gave such practices legal value by enjoining 'that all put their trust in God's judgment'. Little did it matter

---

[8]Many examples are given in P. Riché, *La vie quotidienne dans l'Empire carolingien* (Paris: 1973) 215–226.
[9]Texts translated from Vogel, *Le pécheur*, p.87.
[10]*Ibid.*, p.89.

that some prelates, especially Agobard, archbishop of Lyon, and even Popes Nicholas I and Stephen V some time later, condemned ordeals, stressing the fact that God's judgments are inscrutable; they went unheeded. Better still, new ordeals, christian in appearance, originated, such as proof by consecrated host.

As a matter of fact—and this is an extremely important element for the later development of Christianity—, at the time the spirituality of the clergy and that of the laity did not constitute two worlds cut off from one another. Outside a very small elite of bishops and abbots who strove to remain faithful to patristic tradition and vainly attempted to oppose the ongoing evolution, the clerics shared the same culture—or lack of it—as the laity and were influenced by the surrounding mentality. Thus the Church, which had long entertained reservations about certain directions of popular piety, may be seen to open up during the carolingian period to those which appeared compatible with christian doctrine. In particular, it took over the cult of the dead, as witnessed in the ninth century by the institution of the feast of All Saints; that celebration satisfied an essential demand of popular piety by underlining the call of the faithful departed to salvation. At the same time, under Alcuin's influence, the remembrance of the dead was introduced into the canon of the Mass.

We encounter the same interaction between popular spirituality and that of the churchmen in the cult of the angels and saints. The faithful felt unprotected before God, the faraway and yet omnipresent Judge. They experienced the need to resort to go-betweens. This role was first held by the angels, who loom large in the religious life of the time. They were viewed primarily as heavenly creatures assigned to specific tasks, the main one being the protection of human beings. The archangels, the only ones personalized, were the tutelary spirits of human communities and the wielders of power. The best-known of them, Michael, Gabriel, and Raphael, were granted the honors of a special cult and could be depicted in churches, by virtue of a decision taken by the roman council of 745. Michael and Gabriel are very often found in the iconography of the carolingian period, in association with the central figure of Christ: God is always surrounded and worshiped by a retinue of spiritual beings. The latter two angels were, however, too immaterial to hold much of the faithful's attention. Saint Michael alone, as keeper of paradise and intercessor in favor of men at the last judgment, enjoyed real popularity, as evidenced by the large number of shrines then dedicated to him. In the ninth and tenth centuries, he even took Christ's place in narthex chapels, previously reserved to the worship of the Saviour.

This is only one example of the growing importance assumed by the cult of the saints in the piety of the period. In fact, the faithful were less interested in the virtues of God's servants, stressed by hagiographical literature of exclusively clerical origin, than in their powers. Their relics—that is, parts of their bodies or even objects which had been in contact with them during their life or even after their death—were passionately sought after. Touching them or simply approaching the tomb or reliquary containing them was, for the faithful, a privileged opportunity of coming into contact with the other world and especially of capturing the beneficial dynamism issuing from it to their own advantage, in order to obtain victory or healing. The clerics, besides, did not lag behind in rushing to Rome to buy or steal remains of martyrs in large numbers—those remains of which some parts of christendom were unfortunately deprived. All of this occasioned serious abuses, which the carolingian bishops attempted to limit by laying the foundations of a discipline regarding the cult of relics. Solemn translations of the 'sacred bodies', accompanied by religious ceremonies, were multiplied. Lay people flocked to them in droves, convinced as they were that the influence of the precious remains became more effective when they were lifted off the ground and transferred from one place to another. Most important, the Church granted the sanctoral cycle more prominence in the liturgy. Reciting the litanies of the saints became common practice at Saint Peter's in

Rome during the eighth century; Alcuin later introduced those litanies into the monastic office. The cycle of feasts was considerably enriched by comparison to that of the early centuries of Christianity: in addition to feasts of the Virgin, the anniversaries of the apostles and evangelists, of the Holy Innocents and of Saint Martin and the feasts of the dedication and of the patrons of each church came to be celebrated everywhere. In many places, Michaelmas, the feast of Saint Lawrence, and the Finding of the Cross were also solemnized as early as this time. This last devotion was particularly dear to monks, and Alcuin, who had a special veneration for the instrument of salvation, wrote an office of the Holy Cross.

Generally speaking, the Church strove to christianize the atmosphere of diffuse sacredness with which popular religion surrounded the main events of life. Thus, alongside the eucharistic liturgy, all sorts of parallel liturgies appeared, the most important being blessings and exorcisms.[11] The former concerned food and the implements of work. Special formulas were recited over water, bread, wine, oil and fruit, boats, fishnets, and so on. Others ensured protection against natural calamities, wild animals, or the dangers of travel. Candles blessed on the feast of Saint Blaise were a safeguard against thunder and hail. Finally, illness and especially madness were countered by exorcisms, accompanied by signs of the cross aimed at driving out the devil, the author of all physical and moral evil. By means of these proliferating rites, the Church sought to permeate the daily existence of the faithful with religion. It succeeded only too well, for the latter were led to assign such rituals magic power and to afford them as much if not more importance as the sacraments properly so called.

The risk of deviation was no imaginary one. This readily appeared in the case of ordeals. These ceremonies, whose origin was lay (that is, pagan), were surrounded with liturgical forms

[11]Cf. A. Franz, *Die kirchlichen Benediktionen im Mittelalter*, 2 vol. (1909).

as early as the ninth century. They were usuallly preceded by
a Mass, after which the objects to be used in the judgment
of God were blessed. Everywhere but in Rome, where they
were not in favor, ordeals were accepted by the clergy. Trial by
fire was prominent in carolingian hagiography; for instance, it
allowed Saint Richarda to prove her virginity. As late as the beginning of the twelfth century, the bishops of northern France
resorted to trial by water to confound heretics: the accused
were thrown into a deep pool, and those whom the waters cast
away were exposed as guilty to popular vengeance. At the end-
point of this development, no distinction remained between
the profane and the sacred: the clergy itself was unable to give
a strict definition of the latter. The royal coronation did not
differ in nature from the consecration of the body of Christ:
everything was 'sacrament' (*sacramentum*).

In such an atmosphere of undifferentiated sacredness, there
could be no question of inner life as we understand it. Man
entered into connection with the supernatural by means of
formulas and especially of gestures, through which his various
feelings were expressed. Ritual signs within the liturgy itself
may be seen to proliferate during this period. Some—such
as priest beating his breast at the *Confiteor*—simply exteriorized the meaning of the words being spoken. But other
elements of this gestural symbolic system—such as extended
arms during the reading of the Canon, or the many signs
of the cross and kissings of the altar which punctuatued
the main phases of the Mass—evidence a concern for direct
communication with God. Generally speaking, the forms and
significance of the act of worship underwent an evolution.
Dramatic depictions which focused on spectacular episodes in
the life of Christ took on growing prominence. In the *ludi* or
sacred games composed by monks, the best example of which
is the famous *Whom seek ye in the sepulchre?* (*Quem queritis
in sepulchro*), the laying of his body to rest, his resurrection
and the discovery of the empty tomb by the holy women on
Easter morning were mimed. The introduction of dialogued
sequences and of alternating questions directed attention to

the historical narrative, presented under its more picturesque aspect, rather than to meditation on the paschal mystery. The manner of celebrating the latter moreover underwent significant developments: the ceremonies which took place from Holy Thursday to Easter morning centered no longer on the triumphal celebration of the Saviour's resurrection, but on his crucifixion and burial. 'Symbol, overlaid as it was with confused speculation', writes C. Heitz, 'was obliterated. The shift was towards allegory and humanization of the godly. From the mystery formerly received through the secret paths of symbolic transposition, we move on to historical, and soon to theatrical depiction'.[12]

Under such conditions, it is hardly surprising that the carolingian period should represent a very drab episode in the history of spiritual literature. Precarious living conditions, an insecurity increased by the ninth-century invasions, and finally a low cultural level suffice to account for its rarity and, generally speaking, its mediocrity. Monastic circles were alone in producing a few not inconsiderable works, such as the ascetic treatises of Ambrose Autpert, abbot of Saint Vincent of Volturno (d.784),[13] or the *Diadem of Monks* written by Smaragdus of Saint-Mihiel around 810—and even this latter is no more than an anthology of texts borrowed from the Church Fathers and from Saint Gregory the Great. Admittedly, many hagiographic works were composed in the eighth and ninth centuries, but the notion of sanctity which emerges from them could hardly have nourished and enriched the piety of the faithful. The figures they glorified were most often those of monks or hermits, and were drawn less often than during the previous centuries from the ranks of the secular clergy and bishops. Moreover, their sanctity was presented

[12]C. Heitz, *Recherches sur les rapports entre architecture et liturgie à l'époque carolingienne* (Paris: 1963) 245.
[13]C. Leonardi, 'Spiritualità di Ambrogio Autperto', *Studi medievali*, 3d series, 9 (1968) 1–131.

as a virtue acquired both by heredity—most of the saints of
the carolingian period stemmed from aristocratic families—
and by divine predestination. Permanently invested by grace,
they appear as exceptional beings whom one does not tire
of admiring, but who can by no means be imitated. In short,
they are spiritual meteorites rather than models. Not that their
observances stand out as excessive. Quite the contrary. They
are marked by a sense of moderation, and the devil has only
a limited place in their lives. But they have been chosen by
God to be saints, just as others have been predestined for
damnation, and the human will can do nothing about it. It
is significant, for that matter, that one of the rare theological problems which gave rise to passionate and prolonged
controversy in the ninth century was that of predestination,
brought up by the saxon monk Gottschalk. The latter, push-
ing Saint Augustine's already pessimistic views on the matter
still further, stated that every human person was particularly
predestined to life or death. Condemned as a heretic in 848,
he was nevertheless supported by many abbots and bishops,
and not until 860 was a synod able, at Hincmar's instigation,
to come up with a compromise formulation which, without
denying the divine foreknowledge, underscored the saving
will of God and the universal nature of redemption. But the
bitter discussions which pitted clerics against one another on
this occasion bring out how difficult it was, even for the best
minds of the time, to conceive of the role of human freedom
and the action of grace.

Moreover, the commonly-held notion of God as sovereign
judge and transcendant power favored reverent fear rather
than outpourings of the heart. Even eschatological anticipation, so prominent during the first centuries of Christianity,
seems to lose its intensity in carolingian times, at least outside
monastic circles. Admittedly, eighth and ninth-century clerics
were well acquainted with the Book of Revelation, commentaries on which were written in Spain by Beatus of Liebana, in
Italy by Ambrose Autpert and in the frankish world by Alcuin
and Walafrid Strabo. But it is striking to note that among the

themes conveyed by that prophetic book, most of the authors of the time were primarily sensitive to that of the heavenly Jerusalem viewed as an ideal model of the Church. Far from being a source of worry or anxiety, reflection on the world's future reinforced in them the certainty that there existed in history, as in the physical universe, an order set by Providence. In this perspective, the Second Coming appeared less as an elating or tragic event than as the necessary ratification of God's plan for creation. Such a spirituality inspired the clerics' way of acting, or else it was a reflection of it. The best of them devoted all their energies to restoring regular observance and a dignified celebration of worship. On the whole, the Church of the time seemed less intent on the Saviour's return in glory than concerned with contributing, in its own sphere, to achieving the carolingian monarchs' grand design of making the maxim of order prevail everywhere.

Between the eighth and tenth centuries, a certain concept of the christian faith, characterized by the dimension of mystery and by anticipation of the last times, finally disappeared. It gave way to a set of representations and practices whose inspiration was noticeably different. The historian cannot be content to view this process as no more than a deterioration of religious spirit—a not uncommon attitude. Rather than passing value judgments, it is incumbent on him to note that the impact of Christianity on uncultivated and concrete minds gave rise to a new way of relating to the godly. The discovery of the historical Christ, the valorization of moral life, the importance afforded rituals and gestures constitute the foundations of a spirituality which was to unfold fully in the course of the following centuries.

II

THE MONASTIC
AND FEUDAL AGE
From the Late Tenth to the Eleventh Century

IN THE POLITICAL SPHERE, the decades which preceded and followed the year 1000 were marked by the breakup of the carolingian political system—a process more or less rapid from one area to another—and by the emergence of the new feudo-vassalic institutions. These decades approximately constitute what Marc Bloch has called 'the first feudal age'. In the field of religion, this period may be characterized by the growing influence exercised by monastic spirituality on the christian people as a whole. These two sets of occurrences were not unrelated: the Church of carolingian times was primarily a secular Church, ruled by the monarch and by the bishops who had authority over the monks of their dioceses. As a result of the great upheavals which took place in the West between the end of the ninth century and the middle of the tenth, the priestly order fell into deep decay. The process of secularization, which had begun as early as the ninth century, quickened with the rise of feudalism. Church property was often squandered by unworthy prelates or claimed by envious laymen, and the lifestyle of clerics became increasingly similar to that of the faithful. Most bishops, born in aristocratic circles and brought to office for primarily political and economic reasons, lived like great lords and behaved like potentates rather than churchmen. Even when they preserved some moral dignity—which was often the case in the Empire at the time of the Ottonians—they were completely taken up by the management of their estates and by the political responsibilities entrusted to them by monarchs and men in high places. The rural clergy, largely made up of serfs freed in order to serve as ministers of worship in the churches built by their lords, shone neither by morals nor by education. Many priests were married, whether formally or by common law. Most of them practised a trade: in the countryside, they tilled the lands which made up the parish glebe and lived in the midst of the peasantry. In the cities, as may be observed, for instance, in Milan in the middle of the ninth century, they engaged in all sorts of secular activities: money-dealing, gambling, hunting, and so on. The program imposed on the urban clergy by the carolingian reformers, which called for a common life, had not been completely abandoned, but in many places community discipline slackened considerably.

These developments also affected the monasteries. Many of them, entrusted to lay abbots or exploited by unscrupulous minor nobles, did not escape decline. Yet monasticism was the institution which best resisted the severe crisis then challenging the very existence of the Church, threatened as it was with dissolution both by the secularization of the clergy and by the spread of the private-church system. In the heart of the dark ages, abbeys such as Sankt Gallen, Monte Cassino or Saint-Riquier succeeded, albeit laboriously, in maintaining regular observance and a dignified celebration of the divine worship. In any case, the monks were the first to pull themselves together: in Burgundy, where Cluny was founded in 909; in Lorraine where Gorze (from 933 onward) and Brogne (around 950) were active centers of renewal; and finally in England, where Saint Ethelwold's efforts led in 970 to the promulgation of the *Concordance of Rules (Regularis concordia)*, a charter for a unified and reformed monasticism in the Isles. After the year 1000, the movement spread to southern Europe: Saint Victor at Marseilles became the center of an important monastic federation which radiated as far as Italy, whereas under the influence of the abbey of Fruttuaria, near Turin, reform currents penetrated the germanic lands by way of Sankt Blasien and Siegburg. It is worthy of note that these movements did not originate in any central authority, as had been the case of the religious reforms of the carolingian period. Reversion to the fervor of old was not the consequence of an administrative program spelling a return to order, but truly an expression of monastic society's deep-seated longing for spiritual renewal.

In many cases, the monasteries involved had been founded or reformed at the initiative of bishops or lay lords. Indeed, all the Christians of the time were convinced of the eminent dignity of monasticism and of its superiority over other states of life. In an era when building a church was regarded as the most deserving of all actions, installing in it a religious community whose prayer would be pleasing to God seemed especially indicated. Such spiritual motivations were reinforced by others, connected with the social and political conditions of the post-carolingian West. At the time of Charlemagne and his immediate successors, owning and founding monasteries was one of the monarchs' prerogatives. In royal or imperial abbeys, such as Saint-Denis, Farfa or Fulda, prayers were offered for them to God. Those who headed the territorial principalities erected, from the tenth century onward, on the ruins of the carolingian empire made this royal prerogative, like all others, their own: in Normandy and Flanders, as in Catalonia or in the duchy of Benevento, imposing monasteries rose up, evidencing for all to see the power of the henceforth autonomous dukes and earls.

Moreover, the new society which was being built up within the feudal framework adopted the ideology of the three states of life, first mentioned precisely during the tenth century. According to Adalbero, bishop of Laon, who, early in the eleventh century, provided an especially clear formulation of this global vision of the relationship between social groups, the christian people was one in God's eyes by virtue of the baptism which all had received; but if one referred to the

organization of the earthly city, it in fact included three
'orders': the *oratores* who prayed, the *bellatores* who fought,
and the *laboratores* who worked. Each of these groups fulfilled
a specific role, and none of them could survive without the
others. In this interdependent society based on functional
tripartition, the clergy held a choice place: it was named
first, which indicated a preeminence of honor. From our
perspective, however, it is more interesting to note that this
classification sanctioned the social usefulness of prayer as vital
to the world's survival and salvation. Although its earliest
formulations are to be found in texts written by bishops,
the three-part scheme was to prove especially favorable to
monks, who, in the eyes of the men of that time, were those
who prayed most and best. To the degree that it made the
specialists of prayer into an *ordo*, such a taxonomy reflected
a tendency characteristic of the mentality of the period. This
consisted in making things religious into a separate category,
set apart from 'profane' life. The true religious men (*viri
religiosi*) were those Christians who lived apart from the world
and sanctified themselves by giving thanks and praise to God.
During the feudal age, the main spiritual centers of the West
were communities of men and women who together practised
Christianity with a degree of perfection to which the common
faithful could not attain. Henceforth and until the thirteenth
century, all spiritual movements within the Church were to
have the foundation of religious orders as their starting point
or end-point.

Not only did the three-part scheme assign value to the
office of prayer; it also defined two different categories within
the laity, warriors and workers, or, to speak in terms of the
social reality of the time, lords and peasants. The fact that the
former were named before the latter in the hierarchy of roles
was by no means fortuitous: such a classification confirmed
that, whereas in the christian society of feudal times clerics
came before lay people, among the latter lords preceded their
underlings. Such precedence was by no means theoretical,

since those who wielded power in this world enjoyed a privileged place in church, both in life when attending Mass and after their death at burial. And did the priest not come up to the local lord every Sunday at the end of the service to have him kiss the corporal? More deeply, basic religious attitudes were marked by the ascendancy of the feudal class which, even in the spiritual sphere, imposed its models on society as a whole. The very attitude of prayer which became current between the tenth and twelfth centuries—hands folded—reproduced the gesture by which the vassal paid homage to his lord. As for the investiture ritual for bishops or abbots, it became so similar to that of investiture for fiefs that the one was finally put on a par with the other.

While sharply set off from the working masses, the lay aristocracy lived in close symbiosis with the clergy, and especially with the monks. Lords and religious had in common the fact that they were the masters of the land and did not work with their hands. Moreover, most choir monks stemmed from noble families. In many monasteries, children offered by their parents—that is, oblates—were accepted only with a dowry; also, the ability to read Latin implied an education, which was available at the time only in lordly circles—with a few illustrious exceptions. Abbeys and monasteries thus became refuges for the younger sons and daughters of aristocratic lineages; the girls found in the monastic institution a solution to their inheritance problems. Finally, the Church considered that noble blood conferred sacred prestige and created a natural predisposition to sanctity: 'those who are well-born are unlikely to degenerate' in religious life, to quote an eleventh-century monastic chronicler.[1] All these indications provide a measure of the close bonds uniting lordly circles with the world of the cloister. Their meeting gave birth to a spirituality both monastic and feudal which marked the religious life of

[1] *Quedlimburg Annals*, MGH SS 3:54.

western society in an exclusive manner until the end of the twelfth century and one whose impact was to make itself felt until the end of the Middle Ages.

MONASTIC SPIRITUALITY

During the tenth and eleventh centuries, all western monks followed the Rule of Saint Benedict. This makes it possible to speak of monasticism as an entity. In practice, this did not exclude some flexibility, or even relative diversity from one abbey to the next, for the Rule's adaptation to local conditions and to the founders' intentions was ensured by customaries which organized daily life in concrete terms. But the main principles and the forms of religious life were laid down by the venerated and untouchable benedictine rule. This monolithism, imposed by carolingian legislation, was perfectly suited to an as yet simple and static society.

Prayer and Liturgy: The Example of Cluny

The fascination exercised by monastic life and spirituality is very understandable in a civilization for which the primary religious act was worship offered to God. As Marc Bloch wrote,

> in this christian society, no office performed in the public interest seemed more vital than that of spiritual bodies. Let us make no mistake: inasmuch as they were spiritual. The charitable, cultural, and economic role of the great cathedral chapters and of the monasteries may well have been, in fact, considerable. In the eyes of their contemporaries, it was no more than accessory.[2]

The monastery, that true citadel of prayer, was the place above all others where God was worshipped.

---

[2]Marc Bloch, *La société féodale* (1939) 1:139. English translation *Feudal Society*, 2 vols. (Chicago: University of Chicago Press) 1961, 1964.

That had not always been the case; Saint Benedict himself had not given the liturgical life a privileged place. In his eyes, the monk was primarily a penitent who had entered religious life in order to weep over his sins and place himself under the spiritual direction of the abbot. Not until carolingian times had the office of prayer become dominant in monasticism, and that due especially to Benedict of Aniane. It was left to the early feudal age, and particularly to Cluny, to push this tendency to its ultimate consequences. That burgundian monastery, founded in 910 by Abbot Berno with the help of Duke William of Aquitaine, was not long in extending its influence to a good part of the West, from England to Italy. Directly linked to the Church of Rome, it was the most important religious congregation in christendom from the end of the tenth century to the beginning of the twelfth, and, thanks to a series of remarkable abbots, its impact on all spheres of society was considerable. Of course, monasticism in the feudal era did not amount to Cluny alone. Far from it. Other spiritual traditions remained very much alive, particularly in Germany and Italy. But it is by no means excessive to view Cluny as the most authentic expression of feudal society's spiritual aspirations.

Although the Cluniacs were Benedictines like other monks of the time, the rhythm and the organization of their life were to a large degree original. For instance, whereas Saint Benedict had set the number of psalms to be recited each day at forty, by the end of the eleventh century the daily figure at Cluny was two hundred and fifteen. The Rule called for reading the psalter once each week. In Abbot Odilo's day, the entire Bible had to be read in the course of a year.[3] Lastly, the founder's provisions instituted an approximate balance between the various aspects of monastic life: four hours for the reading of sacred texts and church authors (*lectio divina*),

[3]Ph. Schmitz, 'La liturgie de Cluny', in *Spiritualità cluniacense* (Todi: 1960) 83-99.

three and a half hours for the liturgy, and six hours for work. In cluniac monasteries, the last was reduced to a few symbolic and very brief activities, the best part of the religious' time being devoted to liturgical prayer and to the meditated reading of Scripture.

This predominance of public worship, termed the 'work of God' (*Opus Dei*), was especially manifest in the lengthening of the office. Very long lessons—excerpts from biblical and patristic texts—came to be inserted between the sung parts. Moreover, granted that Cluny did not invent supererogatory offices (that is, additional services not required by the Rule), it did make them into a general practice which spread throughout the houses of its allegiance; versicles and collects were added to the psalms, as happened, for instance, in the *Trina oratio* recited in honor of the Trinity. There was also a proliferation of suffrages (consisting of an antiphon, a versicle, and a collect) and litanies. Finally, the liturgy was enriched with gestures and actions aimed at accentuating its dramatic character: some of the psalms were recited sitting on the ground, and when the Gospel of the Passion was read on Good Friday two monks took hold of pieces of cloth laid on the altar and tore them up at the words, 'They shared out his clothing among them'. The office was also extended in space, and liturgy became pilgrimage: as early as the ninth century, at Saint-Riquier, the monks went in procession on the great feasts from the abbey church to another chapel. At Cluny, a solemn procession led the monks twice daily from the basilica to the church of Saint Mary, where Vespers was sung.

Besides the office chanted in choir, Mass held an important place in the monks' life and spirituality. At Cluny, there were two daily conventual Masses: the morning Mass celebrated at Saint Mary's, and the high Mass sung at the main altar in the basilica after Sext. Here again, liturgical amplifications were possible and frequent: the sung *Introït* repeated three times, the development of the *Kyrie*, and especially the addition to the *Alleluia* of a prose and sequence; the latter were verse texts which glossed in lyrical terms the meaning of the mystery emphasized in the day's liturgy. Add to this the private Masses said by those monks who were priests—the majority in the great abbeys. On account of this it had become necessary to increase the number of altars, and therefore of side chapels surrounding the ambulatory. These ceremonies were accompanied by censing and sprinkling holy water. All this created a sacred atmosphere which was intended to give the soul direct access to the supernatural through the splendor of the celebrations. Individual prayer was not neglected, and the religious were not obliged to participate simultaneously in all the services. But liturgical and community prayer remained central: squadrons of monks followed one another in choir like battalions on the firing line, seeking to offer God uninterrupted praise and a sacrifice pleasing to him. Only the achievement of this grand design could justify the ever heavier burden of ritual observances.

In the monastic spirituality of the feudal era, liturgical prayer was an act not only of praise, but also of intercession and petition. Indeed, around the year 1000 a spectacular increase in the number of votive Masses celebrated for particular intentions can be observed everywhere. At Cluny, the first of the two conventual Masses was always sung for the deceased. At the office of Matins, four psalms were recited for the 'abbey's familiars', others for the king, and on it went. In particular, more and more prayers were offered for the dead, and whole parts of the office were said for them. It was, in fact, Abbot Odilo who, at the end of the tenth century, instituted the feast commemorating the faithful departed, or All Souls' Day, on 2 November. Moreover, there were prayer chains between monasteries: they sent one another their obituaries, setting down on them the names of monks who had just died in associated abbeys so that they would be mentioned in their intercessions. Lay benefactors—rulers or great lords— could also be recorded there. This was a coveted honor, which well deserved the considerable financial sacrifices made to that purpose, particularly in the form of pious donations. In order to ensure this office of intercession over the world, the monks sought help and support. Hence the growing importance of the liturgical cult of the saints: at Cluny, the gregorian sanctoral was enriched by the addition of numerous offices for french saints; the office of All Saints was recited daily, and high Mass was preceded by the reading of the litanies. On a saint's feast day, his passion—if a martyr was involved—or in the case of a confessor, his life was read in its entirety. The text to be read on that occasion—the *legenda*, which is the meaning of the word 'legend'—took up the first eight lessons of matins, where the saints' prayers were most particularly requested.

In the last analysis, the meaning of this both solemn and exuberant liturgy can be understood only by envisioning liturgical prayer as a weapon. The monk used it first of all against himself, in order to fight temptations and especially *acedia*, that spiritual weariness which threatened those who longed for perfection more than it did others. By manfully following the narrow path of regular observance, he could, however, elude the snares laid by the 'Ancient Foe', the devil. It then remained for him to carry on the daily struggle of snatching as many souls as possible from damnation and everlasting fire by means of prayer. This constant battle against the forces of evil bore various spiritual fruits which benefited the christian community by the revertibility of merits: the repose of their souls ensured to the departed and in particular to the souls in purgatory, peace for the living, the fertility of the earth, victory for kings and founder-princes. The monastery, that school of divine service, was also the place at which were won, by dint of prayer, supernatural graces in which all of society shared.

Angelic Life and Contempt of the World

We would be giving an inaccurate view of tenth and eleventh-century monastic spirituality were we to note only the place held in it by prayer and the struggle against the forces of evil. For another reason as well, the life of the cloister appeared to the men of that time superior to all the great and good things the world had to offer: it was a privileged state which allowed creatures to return to their Creator by faithfully serving him. Such communion with the citizens of heaven would be achieved, of course, only at the end of time, but it began already in this world. As Jean Leclercq has aptly demonstrated,[4] the medieval monk was impelled by longing for God and for the heavenly homeland. Through liturgical prayer, he strove to join his voice to the heavenly choirs; by the practice of asceticism and mortification, he sought to lead an angelic life, far removed from the pleasures and temptations of this world. The monastery where regular observance was practised became an anticipation of paradise, a bit of heaven on earth.

This eschatological dimension of monasticism allows us to understand the place occupied in its spirituality by reading and meditating on the Bible. The Old Testament played an important part in this inasmuch as it was viewed as prefiguring the ultimate phase of salvation history inaugurated by the Incarnation: in relation to the Parousia, that is, Christ's glorious coming at the end of time, the people of God found itself in the same situation as the Israël of old had been with regard to the coming of the Messiah in the flesh. The history of the jewish people, however, was seen as a source not so much of moral models—as it had been in carolingian times—as of spiritual attitudes attuned to the climate of tension surrounding the last things which characterized the religious life of the monks of the period. For the cloistered this was by no means a literary theme. The quest for God came within the scope of their daily agenda: the goal of *lectio divina* was, after all, to lead the mind to meditation in order to bring it, even here below, to the contemplation of the divine mystery.

[4]Especially in his great work, *L'Amour des lettres et le désir de Dieu* (Paris: 1957); ET: *The Love of Learning and The Desire for God*, translated Catherine Misrahi (New York: 1961).

Eschatological anticipation also expressed itself among monks in a will to personal and collective purification which gave rise to most of the reform movements of the time. Great abbots like William of Volpiano or Saint Peter Damian were impelled by the desire to make the world of the cloister into a perfect society, a true anticipation here below of the kingdom of God. Such a tendency evidenced itself with particular clarity at Cluny during the eleventh century. It is no misuse of language to term cluniac spirituality triumphalistic, for notions of sin and redemption were far less familiar to it than the contemplation of the divine glory and majesty. It was certainly not by chance that Saint Hugh had removed from the *Exultet* the words: 'happy fault!' (*O felix culpa!*), that paradoxical celebration of Adam's offense as the starting point of Redemption. In a spiritual climate more imbued with the spirit of the Transfiguration than with that of the Incarnation, a climate in which the monastery was seen as the anteroom of heaven, the meaning of such supernatural realism was no longer understood. Cluny's artistic conceptions, and those of the black monks in general, were a product of the same mindset: nothing was too beautiful or too luxurious for God's house, where the brilliance of gold, the glitter of lights, and the scent of incense converged to give those who entered it a foretaste of the splendors of the heavenly court.

Considering themselves as they did to be the vanguard of the people of God which had already reached the gates of the Kingdom, monks sometimes experienced a tendency to disparage other states of life within the Church. Convinced they possessed the tokens of salvation, they called on the best Christians, and particularly on high-placed laymen, to join them in the peace of the cloister and embrace monastic life. Thus a new spiritual aristocracy formed within the abbeys, one that, sofar as its members' origins were concerned, differed little from that which, during the same period, imposed its authority on the lowborn members of secular society.

We can thus grasp why many medieval spiritual texts present entering the cloister as an event as important as baptism, if not more so. Was the monastery not both a memorial of the historical Jerusalem, even in some of its architectural elements, and a prefiguration of the heavenly one? Be that as it may, its inhabitants shared the dignity of the sons of Zion and enjoyed the graces proper to places sanctified by the Lord's life. The conversion implied by religious profession was experienced as a surpassing of one's earthly condition. To become a monk was both to return to the original state of perfection and to anticipate the life to come; it also spelled a refusal of the world for the purpose of building the new man called to take his place at God's side.

The reverse side of such a yearning for the things on high was the tendency to despise those here below—something very marked among most spiritual writers of the time. Some studies, particularly those of R. Bultot, have insistently emphasized this systematic disparagement of temporal and carnal realities, which went much further than a mere warning against abuses resulting from an immoderate use of the things of this world. Saint Anselm, John of Fécamp, Bernard of Morlaas and many others advocated contempt for the world (*contemptus mundi*) in their treatises and passed a basically pessisimistic judgment on temporal realities, earthly activities, and human love, which means on secular life as a whole. Conversely, these same writers extolled monastic life, presented as the authentic form of christian experience and the sole path to salvation. In their eyes, the world was fraught with illusions and occasions of sin. It was better therefore to give up creatures and to live on earth as a pilgrim and a stranger: the Kingdom was won through exile. Eleventh-century spiritual writers were convinced that there was an absolute incompatibility between religious life and the concerns, occupations or business of the world. The peace of the cloister and regular discipline alone could guarantee *otium*, that tranquillity which made the inner life possible.

Such a world-view rested on absolute theocentrism: since God stood for all that was good, there was no point in pursuing earthly goals, which were doomed to disappointment

and carried with them the danger of sin: 'Sensitive solely
to the disproportion between God and finite being', Bultot
writes, 'monastic spirituality disqualified the latter in the order
of values, without questioning itself as to the essence and
meaning peculiar to it'.[5] The condemnation of the 'world',
a major theme of Saint John's Gospel, was interpreted by
monastic writers as a negative judgment passed on the whole
of creation.

Such misgivings, to say the least, about human affairs may
seem surprising to a twentieth-century person, especially if
he or she refers, for the sake of comparison, to some of the
Second Vatican Council's basic decrees. The historian's role
consists, not in contrasting modern texts with those written
by monks of feudal times, but in attempting to understand
and explain their contradictions, which are more than just
apparent. It is essential in this regard to realize that eleventh-
century spiritual authors were dependent on their own reading of the Bible: in the Vulgate, scriptural contrasts were
hardened and impoverished by inadequate translations. Thus
the semitic antithesis between the Flesh and the Spirit was
reduced to an antagonism between body and soul, whereas
in actual fact it covers much more complex realities. Too
often, moreover, they undiscerningly adopted as their own
the philosophical notions of the ancient world conveyed by
patristic literature, such as the definition of asceticism as a
search for insensitivity, inspired by Stoicism rather than by
the Gospel, or the platonic opposition between contemplation
and action. The sorry state of medieval culture did not allow
for the selectivity necessary within this mixed heritage.

Moreover, some basic concepts of monastic spirituality
were not devoid of ambiguity: was the 'angelic life' so highly
extolled by spiritual writers simply a longing for unity in God,
or did it also involve a refusal of the human condition, and

[5]R. Bultot, 'Spirituels et théologiens devant l'homme et le monde',
Revue thomiste 64 (1964) 546.

particularly of sexuality? By taking literally various passages from Saint Augustine—one of the most widely read authors of the time—, some monks occasionally let themselves be carried along on the slope towards gnosticism and even towards dualism, to which their ascetic ideal inclined them. For they regarded the world as no more than a reality devoid of any consistency of its own, a mere debased reflection of a celestial world in which truth was to be found. In considering its history, they were less attentive to what was being built up than to what was bringing it closer to its end. As the realm of transiency and contingency, created being was to give rise not to attachment or even to regard, but to contempt and flight. By repudiating the earthly world, eleventh-century monastic spirituality projected evil outside man, as it were, and located it in things, thus conferring an objective, imposing reality on it. Far from quashing the foe, this succeeded only in reinforcing its hold on human minds.

We must, however, qualify what may appear absolute and peremptory in the judgments on the world, which a good number of monastic spiritual authors expressed, by considering the motives which guided them. Indeed, irrevocable condemnations of earthly realities usually occur in a context of controversy. Most writings on contempt for the world date from the eleventh century or the beginning of the twelfth, a time at which the struggle against simony was a major concern, and secular values were held in high enough honor by simoniac clerics without it being necessary to remind them of their importance. Moreover, at the heart of the battle waged by the living forces of the Church in order to tear it from the grip of the emperors and from feudal disintegration, the flight from the world advocated by monks appeared less as an evasion from life in society and temporal action than as a judgment passed on certain oppressive structures which stood in the way of religious development and of charity. In that case, contempt for the world (*contemptus mundi*) often expressed 'a refusal to compromise with a society which was

perhaps less christian than the most secular of our states'.[6]
Saint Anselm, for instance, authored a treatise on the subject
in which he severely criticized the domestication of prelates
by the king of England and the uncontrolled violence of
the knights. In this specific case, 'contempt for the world'
expressed rejection of a given society rather than a systematic
disparagement of secular realities.

We must also ask ourselves what the world could have
meant to a man of early feudal times, independently of
any ideological influence conveyed by culture. Wherever he
turned, he was surrounded by violence and injustice, and it
was extremely difficult for him to detect any positive values
within secular society: few marriages were based on love, there
was not as yet any lay culture worthy of the name, nor was
there any technical or scientific progress. The state itself was
less the political form assumed by the temporal city than a
sacred order culminating in the person of the emperor or
king, the Lord's anointed and his representative on earth.
The famous investiture controversy which pitted popes against
germanic monarchs during the late eleventh and early twelfth
centuries, was not—as is too often stated—a conflict between
spiritual power and lay authority, but an all-out struggle between two rival sacred orders. In a world whose order was
established by Providence and whose political and social organization was ruled by transcendent models, the very notion of
'temporal' was meaningless. The monks can therefore hardly
be blamed for having been unable to develop a spirituality for
lay people, 'since there was no laity, for lack of a world in
which its specificity could have been grasped'.[7]

And finally, in practice, neither monks nor even hermits—
though the latter seem to have practised contempt for the

[6]J. Batany, 'L'Eglise et le mépris du monde', *Annales E.S.C.* 20 (1965)
218-228.
[7]L.-J. Bataillon and J.-P. Jossua, 'Le mépris du monde. De l'intérêt
d'une discussion actuelle', *Revue des Sciences philosophiques et théologiques*
51 (1967) 23-38.

world literally—were totally foreign or hostile to human society. The indisputable disparagement of earthly realities in monastic spirituality was often tempered by a deep feeling for things and people. The abbeys of feudal times did not cut themselves off from social life: in the great germanic monasteries and even in small priories in France, many children of the aristocracy received an elementary education, without necessarily being destined for a church career. Cluniac spirituality, moreover, required man, not to give up being himself, but to dedicate his life to God's service. As was most aptly put by Étienne Gilson, 'Cluny takes us as we are, less as souls than as human persons, and it is with the help of our bodies, not without them, that it intends to save us'.[8] In this perspective, taking man as he was meant not expecting ascetic feats or excessive mortifications from him; it also meant deciding that wealth, power and beauty, far from being obstacles to the love of God in themselves, can contribute to the praise of his glory and the service of his cause. Thus, following an early, rigoristic phase, the Cluniacs' attitude toward the society of their time was marked by a concern for understanding and openness. This latter was favored by the bonds of kinship and solidarity which were not long in forming between the abbots of the mother house and those in high places, whose action they strove to influence. But the liking—with overtones of leniency—that they showed for lay people was not limited to the ruling classes: Abbot Odilo took an important part in the spread of the peace movement, and we must not forget that Abelard, pursued by Saint Bernard, found a home where he might die in peace near Peter the Venerable; the letter which Peter wrote Heloise to tell her of her husband's death is, moreover, a masterpiece of thoughtfulness and humanity.

Such a confrontation between the theory and practice of monastic attitude towards the world allows us to perceive how complex the problem is. On the one hand, it shows that there

[8]E. Gilson, 'Le message de Cluny', in *A Cluny* (Dijon: 1950) 30.

was a coherent spiritual doctrine equating christian perfection with an ideal of retreat from earthly life and rejection of some aspects of the human condition: angelic life, paradise recovered away from the world, a purely contemplative existence. On the other hand, the eleventh-century monks' concern with interaction with the society around them comes to light—a concern which sometimes went as far as unqualified acceptance of that society's values and structures. In actual fact, the two attitudes are not contradictory. When it comes to changing the world, leaving it may at times be more effective than staying within it, and one sometimes finds man better by running from the crowd than by remaining in its midst. Is it by chance that many abbots—and especially those of Cluny—acted as arbitrators in the political conflicts of the period, both at the local level and at that of christendom? As for the hermits who took refuge deep in the woods in order to flee the world, all historians are now aware of their role in clearing land for cultivation, as well as in establishing roads, assisting travelers and bringing the Gospel to rural populations. This is a measure of how difficult it is to arrive at a fair assessment of a spirituality which, in practice, often gave value to those very realities which it belittled at the level of principle.

THE INFLUENCE OF MONASTIC SPIRITUALITY

Despite all these reservations—and they are sizeable ones—it remains nevertheless true that the monks' ideology had a greater influence on the spirituality of the feudal era than their *praxis.* The monastic ideal exerted an incomparable fascination on all the minds of the time, even the most uncultivated, and some spiritual themes dear to cenobites were taken up again and amplified by others, both clerics or lay people, who carried them to their ultimate consequences.

Secular Life and Religious Life

At that time, indeed, the idea that life in the world was incompatible with the religious state began to prevail among

the Christians of the West. The secular clergy were first to experience the impact of the ascetic doctrines elaborated in the
cloisters, and this modified the very notion of the priesthood.
The eleventh-century monastic reforms had concentrated on
reestablishing the practice of continence in the abbeys. The
steps taken to that effect were not inspired solely by disciplinary considerations. At Cluny, for instance, as early as the
middle of the tenth century, a eucharistic spirituality developed, one focused on adhering to the saving Christ present in
the sacrament of the altar: only by receiving the 'true body of
Christ' could one become a member of his mystical body. But
to approach the Eucharist, and even more to consecrate the
host, purity was an absolute requirement. Odo of Cluny, in his
great poem *Occupatio*, made chastity an absolute necessity for
monks and asserted that the priestly office was incompatible
with concubinage.

When first expressed, these views were looked upon as
daringly ahead of their time. As late as 1010, Bishop Burchard
of Worms, in his penitential entitled *Corrector or Physician*
(*Corrector sive medicus*), provided punishments for lay persons who refused to attend a service celebrated by a married
pastor or one involved in a common-law marriage. But as
early as the second third of the eleventh century, the faithful
everywhere are reported to have questioned the validity of
sacraments dispensed by incontinent priests. In Milan around
1050, the Patarines went further still: they boycotted the
services celebrated by 'nicolaitan' clerics and forced them to
observe chastity, which in their eyes was a basic element of
the priestly state. The gregorian reform made these ideas its
own. It set a new priestly model for several centuries, one
based on an ideal of purity and separation. In Gregory VII's
view, indeed, those who celebrated the sacrifice of the Mass
must be in the image of Christ: the chastity of the Son of
God postulated that of the ministers of worship. Dedicated as
they were to the permanent service of praise offered by Jesus
to the heavenly Father, earthly priests were to live apart from
the faithful and give up whatever might have been secular

about their existence. It was recommended that they lead the common life, which was suited to the office of prayer they had taken on for the entire Church and which, moreover, made it easier to maintain continence. Chastity, life in common, and liturgical service were henceforth the three basic aspects of the priestly state.

Many priests, besides, had modified their lifestyle without waiting for the pope's appeal. As early as the second third of the eleventh century, canonical, that is, community life was restored or instituted in many places, especially in southern areas (for instance at San Freddiano at Lucca, Saint John Lateran and Saint-Ruf near Avignon). Other clerics, faced with the hostility of their colleagues, chose to retire to the desert. Thus, various forms of clerical eremitic life proliferated throughout the West, while the secular clergy as a whole was subjected to the influence of monastic spirituality. That was precisely what the opponents of reform—from the priests of Milan to the Anonymous of York—pointed out in reproaching the papacy for wishing to impose on secular clerics a way of life and moral requirements unsuited to the specific calling of their *ordo*. The argument was not without merit, but since those who put it forth were supported by temporal rulers, they were included in the opprobrium then clouding 'simoniac and nicolaitan' clerics.

The most serious consequence of the spread of monastic spirituality was doubtless a deep and lasting belittling of the lay state. The laity labored under a twofold inferiority, religious and cultural: laity was defined negatively by the fact of being shut out from the realm of the sacred and of scholarly culture. In a world where christian life was identified with consecrated life, the great majority of the baptized were in a less advantageous position than were religious as regarded salvation. The distinction between monks, clerics and laity was of course nothing new in the Church. Gregory the Great, inspired by a passage from the prophet Ezechiel (14:14), had already divided Christians into three categories with reference to ecclesiastical institutions: *conjugati* (married people), *continentes* (religious), *predicatores* (secular clerics). The scheme was taken up again in tenth-century monastic circles, but from a different angle. So it was that shortly before the year 1000, Abbot Abbo of Fleury (Saint-Benoît-sur-Loire) could write:

> Among the faithful of both sexes, we know that there are three orders and, so to speak, three degrees in the holy and universal Church. Although none of the three is free from sin, yet the first is good, the second better, the third excellent. . . . The first is that of lay people, the second that of clerics, the third that of monks.[9]

For this author, as for many of his contemporaries, classifying Christians into types was not aimed solely at singling out three different kinds of existence within the Church. The system was also a hierarchical one, based on the notion of a reward thought to vary according to one's state of life. Referring to the figures given by Christ in the parable of the sower (Mt 13:8) regarding the seed's yield, the spiritual literature of the time clearly rated the superiority of monastic life (100 to 1) over the clerical (60 to 1) and lay (30 to 1) states. Such a scale of values was not universal; throughout the Middle Ages, clerics and monks vied for first place. All agreed, however, on putting the laity at the lowest level. The hierarchy of states of life was based on the assumption that the fleshly condition was evil: the farther one was from the flesh (here identified with sex), the more perfect one was. In such a perspective, marriage, though a sacrament, had no positive value; it was no more than a remedy for concupiscence and a concession to human weakness.[10] Besides, were marital relations not themselves tainted by sin, as Saint Augustine had maintained

[9]Abbo of Fleury, *Apologeticus ad Hugonem et Rodbertum reges Francorum*, PL 139:463.

[10]Abbo, *ibid*.: 'As concerns the married state, it is permitted only for motives of leniency, in order to avoid man's falling into an even worse state at an age at which temptations due to the frailty of the flesh are powerful.'

against Pelagius? In the eschatological perspective to which monasticism remained committed, continence and especially virginity were the foundations of religious life.

This pessimistic view of the condition of lay people and of their role within the Church was not typical of a few isolated or extremist writers. It was shared by the faithful themselves, who saw no way to salvation other than being united as closely as possible with the world of the religious. Knights offered their children to monasteries as oblates. Those who remained in the world affiliated themselves with the most prestigious abbeys in prayer societies or confraternities; in return for pious legacies, which usually took the form of land donations, they gained enrolment in the books containing the names of those for whom the monks prayed daily, and in their obituaries. Although Cluny did not invent such associations, it did develop them considerably, particulary in aristocratic circles. Better still, in the eleventh century the custom of requesting the religious habit on the occasion of a serious illness became widespread among the faithful. The monastic chronicler Ordericus Vitalis gives us a fine example in the person of Ansold of Maule, a former comrade-in-arms of Robert Guiscard. When, after fifty-three years as a knight he felt death near, he addressed his wife in the following terms:

> Odeline, gracious sister and amiable wife, . . . by divine favor we have lived together for over twenty years. Now I am going to my end, and, like it or not, I am approaching death. May it please you to grant me permission to become a monk, and to renounce the pompous raiment of the world in order to put on the black habit of holy father Benedict. Madame, release me, I beseech you, from my marital obligations and commend me faithfully to God so that, rid of the burden of wordly things, I may deserve to receive as insignia the monastic habit and tonsure.

His wife having agreed, he was able to fulfill his wish and was immediately clothed with the habit. Three days later he died, after which 'he was buried with Christ in order to rise with him'.[11] Dying in the monk's habit ensured full and complete participation in the petitions, prayers, and merits of the religious, on the sole condition of renouncing marriage and of divesting oneself of one's 'honors' and goods. For a layman, the threefold rejection of power, sex, and money was the gate to salvation, and it implied the very negation of his state. But the medieval mind, prone to sharp contrasts, knew of none but total conversion. A Christian could hope to please God only by absolute renunciation.

Thus even those who remained in the world out of necessity strove to imitate monastic observance if they had some thought for the hereafter. The *Life of Saint Gerard of Aurillac*, written around the middle of the tenth century by Abbot Odo of Cluny, offers the example of a great lord who attained perfection while living in the world. But let there be no mistake: Saint Gerard by no means embodies an ideal of lay sanctity. Odo constantly presents him as a monk by desire, prevented only by compelling duties from entering the cloister. He depicts him as practising chastity and refusing to resort to arms, for violence is evil in his eyes. When his enemies attack him and he cannot refuse battle, he whirls his sword and pretends to fight while trying not to wound anyone. His religious life is punctuated by an alternation of reading and prayer. Knight though he is, Saint Gerard lives in the world like a monk.[12]

Far from being limited to the upper strata of society, the fascination exercised by the ascetic tendencies of monastic spirituality extended to all lay people in the eleventh century, as we see in the ideology of the peace movements. These did not merely express a longing for the restoration of an order disrupted by feudal anarchy. In the documents produced by the assemblies held between 990 and 1040, precepts

[11]Ordericus Vitalis, *Historia ecclesiastica* II.V.21 (PL 188:443).
[12]Cf. A. Frugoni, 'Incontro con Cluny', in *Spiritualità cluniacense* (Todi:1960) 23-29.

concerning abstinence, along with the rejection of violence, evidence a widespread desire of adopting typically monastic observances. Self-sacrifice practised in common appeared to the men of the year 1000 to be the surest way of deflecting God's wrath and of ensuring the group's salvation. The laity's attachment to monastic institutions and values was, however, no mere phenomenon of imitation or osmosis. It was rather the expression of an awakening of religious consciousness in circles that had theretofore experienced no more than mere conformism. The movement's origins are mysterious: under the influence of the monks, but also of a clergy which, thanks to the decentralized framework of the private-church system, was in closer contact with the faithful, a kind of spiritual penetration—whose forms escape us—took place during those obscure centuries. The lifelessness of the tenth- and eleventh-century religious climate was succeeded by a period of intense fermentation. Ordinary faithful in growing numbers began to attain to some knowledge, if not of the Bible, at least of the main Gospel precepts. Some of them emphasized monastic tradition yet more: in many cases this ended in exaggerated spiritualism. Strikingly enough, the first heresies to appear in the West around the year 1000— those of Vertus in Champagne, of Arras or of Monforte in Lombardy—had in common a refusal of the world and its violence and contempt for the body and for sex, as well as rejection of church structures and of sacraments whose material character they experienced as offensive. We are doubtless dealing only with small groups, quickly reduced to silence by the ecclesiastical hierarchy. But they do seem to express in more radical form the religious aspirations of many people of that time, who, in the name of strict evangelical literalism, tended to erect the highest demands of monastic spirituality into norms of behavior for all Christians. Though they did not go so far, the Patarines of Lombardy or their florentine contemporaries who forced their clergy to embrace celibacy and give up simony shared just this mindset. But far from claiming any kind of spiritual autonomy for themselves, they simply demanded that priests fulfill their role in the Church:

providing the faithful with valid sacraments and offering unto God a sacrifice pleasing to him.

Spiritual Combat

By presenting religious life primarily as a ceaseless struggle against the 'Ancient Foe', monastic spirituality awakened widespread reverberations within a warlike society whose secular ethic (called *ritterliches Tugendsystem* or 'knightly code of virtue' by german authors) favored combat-related values. The view of religious and moral life as a battle between Good and Evil was not, of course, an eleventh-century invention. Prudentius in the patristic era and Alcuin and Smaragdus in carolingian times had afforded the theme of 'psychomachia' a good deal of room in their respective writings. But it was left to the early feudal age—as is evidenced by the sculptures of Moissac and the frescoes of Tavant—to favor this aspect and to make it into the axis of an entire society's spiritual life.

The people of the tenth and eleventh centuries, a period characterized by insecurity and violence, transposed their daily habits and concerns into the religious sphere. According to recent studies founded on a psychoanalytic interpretation, the very structure of the monastic office might have fitted the design of fighting the forces of evil, from whose grasp the monks strove to snatch the souls of the faithful departed by constant and intense prayer. From this perspective, the monastic liturgy, in its sumptuous and solemn setting, would have represented the sublimation of the aggressive impulses of the lay aristocracy, which gave up physical violence only to engage in religious struggle. The knight (*miles*) who entered a monastery left his horse and sword behind, but with a view to gaining a hold on spiritual weapons infinitely more effective than those of the world.[13]

There can be no doubt, in any case, that no epoch took more in earnest than did the Middle Ages the Gospel maxim:

[13]Barbara Rosenwein, 'Feudal war and monastic peace: Cluniac liturgy as ritual aggression', *Viator* 2 (1971) 129-157.

'The kingdom of heaven suffers violence'. The keynote of all spirituality in the feudal period was struggle and painful effort. In monasteries, asceticism was cultivated as a means of returning to God: voluntary suffering allowed man to restore here below the original state of innocence debased by sin, and to attain spiritual freedom. This universally held conviction impelled souls enamored of perfection to seek martyrdom, which, along with the certainty of salvation, provided the merits necessary to the Church and to the faithful departed. For want of persecutors, they inflicted it on themselves. Benedictine asceticism, whose expressions remained moderate, included two basic aspects: the renunciation of sensual pleasures and the struggle against temptations. The second tended to assume growing importance in the eleventh century, as belief in the physical reality of the Devil and his omnipresence developed. The monk Raoul Glaber stated that he had seen Satan several times in the appearance of an unclean beast, and many contemporary saints' lives depict it attacking and thoroughly thrashing those who longed for perfection.

Here again, lay people did not want to be outdone. Many of them, barred by their humble background from becoming monks, embraced the eremitic life, in which they were able to devote themselves to unbridled asceticism. Indeed, with the enthusiasm characteristic of neophytes, they rejected monastic discernment (*discretio*), which in practice tempered the harshness of the prescribed observances, and engaged in an increasing crescendo of mortifications, seeking to exhaust their bodies by fasting and subjecting them to a thousand torments. Such exaggerated severity with oneself was to remain a characteristic feature of the popular spirituality of the Middle Ages from the eleventh-century hermits to the fourteenth-century flagellants, and it is certainly not by chance that those cistercian saints who inflicted the harshest penances on themselves were lay brothers—that is, people of humble station, such as Peter and Nicholas of Villers. It is as though laymen wanted to compensate for their inability to read or meditate on the word of God by wreaking extra violence on their own bodies.

Such a tendency to strive for ascetic performances was, like many spiritual phenomena, deeply ambiguous: it expressed both an anxious obsession with salvation and a longing to imitate the suffering Christ even in his torments, the latter being one of the primary manifestations of evangelical revival. There is no other explanation for the success enjoyed by voluntary flagellation, which developed during the eleventh century in italian eremitic circles, particularly under the influence of Saint Peter Damian. The whip, one of the instruments of Christ's Passion, became a favorite means of penance, securing the ransom of the punishment due for sin for those who struck themselves with it in a process of commutation. But the 'wild' ascetics who proliferated in the West after the year 1000 appeared to seek suffering for its own sake: many hermits and recluses inflicted extraordinary fasts on themselves, or wore hairshirts on their bare skin. Some wound knotted cords or iron bands around their limbs or imprisoned themselves in genuine corsets, like Saint Dominic 'the armored', who, in his retreat at Fonte Avellana, could not move without driving nail-studded metal plates into his flesh. These are extreme forms, but they aptly reflect certain tendencies of the spirituality which was then common. The ideal christian life of feudal times was an heroic one, characterized by a series of tremendous efforts and by the pursuit of records, in the image of the knight who constantly had to surpass himself by performing new feats. Sanctity remained in the realm of the extraordinary, while becoming accessible at the cost of fierce efforts: whoever fasted several weeks in a row, spent his or her nights in prayer and performed miraculous cures was quickly canonized by the masses, if not by the Church.

All the faithful enamored of perfection or simply anxious to ensure their salvation did not, however, become hermits or recluses. There was a less painful way of acquiring some merit in God's eyes, and that was by going on pilgrimage. Already in the early Middle Ages, irish monks had spread by

example a belief in the sanctifying power of religious pere-
grination (*peregrinatio religiosa*), a kind of voluntary exile of
indefinite duration. The significance of pilgrimage changed
in the eleventh century, when large numbers of penitents
chose famous shrines like Santiago de Compostella or holy
places like Rome, and especially Jerusalem, as the goal of their
journey. In an era when travel was a dangerous undertaking,
such long journeys were, understandably enough, considered
by both faithful and clergy an ascetic exercise and a form
of penance. Neither should fasting be omitted from the list
of commendable practices; it was prescribed by the Church
during certain periods of the liturgical year and on certain
days of the week, but could be engaged in more often out of
devotion. Finally, almsgiving was the religious act *par excellence* of the laity, as is stated by one of the earliest legal texts
which attempted to define their status within the Church—
the *Decree* drawn up by the monk Gratian around 1140: 'Lay
people may have a wife, till the earth, judge and bring lawsuits,
lay their offerings on the altar, pay tithes. If they have done
this, they can be saved, provided they avoid vice through the
practice of charity.'

Since our purpose is not to study these pious practices for
their own sake, it will suffice here to bring out their spirit.
Diverse though they were, their aim was identical: the acquisition of merit through hardship and suffering. Medieval people
were deeply convinced that painful atonement alone could
earn them remission of their sins. The main thrust of ascetic
effort was directed against the flesh, and especially against
the body, that favorite ground of evil forces—hence these
attempts to humble it and to break it through mortification.

Such a spirituality, centered around man's struggle against
himself, quite naturally resulted in a religion based on good
works, since the faithful could hope to sway the wrath of
God the Judge solely by multiplying practices of devotion
and charity. When the Arras heretics, in 1025, asserted the
voluntary nature of spiritual regeneration before the bishop
and questioned the value of some sacraments, they did no

more than give an abrupt formulation to the skepticism regarding grace which characterized the religious mentality of their time. It would, however, be a mistake to view such an attitude merely as the expression of a materialistic and unenlightened faith. In fact, the men of feudal times prayed with the means at their disposal: their bodies, their strength, and their courage. As J. Toussaert correctly perceived with respect to the late Middle Ages—although his remark applies equally to the previous centuries—, 'concrete, physical effort replaced the arduous effort of raising one's soul toward God, in a form of piety more exteriorized than ours and very different from it.'[14]

God in History

The main narrative sources at the historian's disposal for the eleventh and twelfth centuries are monastic chronicles; their number and importance witness to the cenobites' marked interest in the course of events. But the abundance of such writings cannot be accounted for solely by a wish to save the past from oblivion and to draw lessons from it. It is also due to the monks' concern with discerning how the work of salvation, inaugurated by the Incarnation, wove itself into the warp of time. Thus medieval chronicles often began with reflections on the creation of the world and with a summary of biblical history before going into an account of the events—sometimes very local ones—which, in our eyes, constitute their true object. For the monks of that time, all particular history was part of the global history of God's people, which was far from over. It was a spiritual man's duty to scrutinize events attentively in order to perceive in them the signs of the Church's growth and of the approach of the *Parousia*. He would remember the episodes he thought most significant,

[14]J. Toussaert, *Le sentiment religieux, la vie et la pratique religieuse des laïcs en Flandre maritime... aux XIVe, XVe et début du XVIe siècle* (Paris: 1963) 247.

and which are not necessarily those that today's historian would like to find.

At their much more down-to-earth level, lay people were no less attentive to the signs of the times. All were deeply convinced that God intervened directly in individual and collective destinies. It was believed, in particular, that his power displayed itself through wonders whose meaning was related to human activities, and that wars and epidemics were consequences of sin. God was identified with immanent justice: he rewarded each according to his deeds. The cluniac chronicler Raoul Glaber recounts how Count Fulk Nera, who had shown his enemies great cruelty, attempted to relieve his conscience by having a church built. On the day of its dedication, a storm broke out in a clear sky and toppled it. No one, we are told, had any doubts as to the significance of the accident.[15] God did not allow events to unfold in a manner contrary to his justice, but before punishing people, he sent them warnings by means of the elements (the stars in particular), and especially through visions and miracles. It was up to each person to heed these and respect them in good time.

The Almighty was not only the keeper of the moral law; he was also the judge who, at the end of the ages, would summon human beings to appear before his court. This judgment, both universal and particular, whose 'day and hour' no one knew, fascinated people's minds at certain periods. In the Middle Ages, and especially in the eleventh century, it was greatly awaited and feared. The Church had penetrated the collective consciousness with the conviction that time was no mere flow, but was directed toward Christ's final return and the coming of the heavenly Jerusalem. The place afforded the Book of Revelation both in monastic spiritual treatises and in romanesque art aptly illustrates how successful the

[15]Raoul Glaber, *Historiae* II.4.32-34, quoted by P. Rousset, 'Raoul Glaber, interprète de la pensée commune au XIe siècle', *Revue d'Histoire de l'Eglise de France* 36 (1950) 5-24.

theme was. Through a natural distortion, the anticipation of the last times gave rise to a whole set of speculations as to the circumstances which were to precede their arrival. As the year 1000 drew near, attention focused especially on the Antichrist, that hundred-faced, ever reborn hydra whose coming the clerics believed they could make out in the vagaries of history: invasions, calamities of various sorts, the appearance of heresies. Adso, a monk of Montier en Der, devoted one of his works to him at the end of the tenth century, and Raoul Glaber refers to him several times. It is more difficult to visualize what kind of notion the ordinary faithful had of him. In any case, until the end of the tenth century, the Christians of the West envisioned the return of the Antichrist as a very real possibility; his persecutions were closely to precede the final judgment. At the news of his appearance in the East, droves of men and women set out unhesitatingly and went off to fight the battles heralding Christ's return in glory.

'The belief in the terrors of the year 1000 is a mistaken one; on the other hand, we must acknowledge that the best Christians of the time lived in a state of latent anxiety and that, meditating on the Gospel, they made this anxiety into a virtue.'[16] Indeed, throughout the eleventh century, the ambivalence of eschatological expectation was clearly apparent: on one hand, it gave rise to pessimistic reactions marked by fear; on the other, especially once the term of the millenium was past, it impelled both faithful and clerics along the way to purification. The religious enthusiasm which accompanied the peace movements and ensured their success, the return of tithes and churches on the part of lords, and finally the rapid development of a renewed monasticism should, it seems, be related to this mindset, marked in the documents of the time by the frequency of the preamble 'With the end of the world approaching' (*Appropinquante fine mundi*). But the momentum aroused by the fearsome approach of the years 1000 and

[16]Georges Duby, *L'an mil* (Paris, 1967) 146.

1033 outlived the circumstances that had given birth to it. During the second half of the eleventh century, both Church and society were to benefit, for their transformation and progress, from the energies that were unleashed as apocalyptic prospects faded gradually into the distance.

FROM REFORM TO CRUSADE:
TOWARD A SPIRITUALITY OF ACTION

Among clerics, eschatological spirituality fostered missionary initiatives—such as those of Bruno of Querfurt or of Saint Adalbert, who undertook to convert the Slavs around the year 1000—and especially reform movements. We have already stressed the close connection between expecting the rapid coming of the Kingdom and longing to present God with a spotless Church. In the eleventh century, the tempo of reform undertakings accelerated. In France, William of Volpiano and Lanfranc, to quote only the greatest, established abbeys, such as Bec and Fécamp, whose cultural and spiritual influence was considerable. In Italy, the movement took the direction of an attempt to combine cenobitic and eremitic livestyles within the framework of the benedictine rule, with such figures as Saint Romuald (d.1027), founder of Camaldoli, and Saint John Gualbert of Vallombrosa (d.1073). Other ecclesiastical circles were touched by a revival of fervor; this was particularly true of some bishops and cathedral chapters in Lotharingia and southern France, which restored the practice of the canonical life. Following vicissitudes which it is not our purpose to study here, all these efforts at recovery led up to the reform of the papacy, which between Nicholas II and Gregory VII gradually shook off the emperor's guardianship and took the lead in the struggle for the freedom of the Church. The sum total of these movements, motley and diverse as they were, has been dubbed 'gregorian reform' by historians, who have thus restricted its import by bringing it down to the action of a single man. Such a denomination is justified, however, if we consider that even before becoming

Pope Gregory VII, the monk Hildebrand had been one of the primer movers and propagators of reform for over thirty years (1049-1084). Having once ascended the apostolic throne, he brought it to its climax. He did not hesitate to lead the Church to the brink of chaos to secure the triumph of the good cause against the supporters of a system considered outrageous. With Humbert of Moyenmoutier, the focus shifted from the struggle against trading in church dignities and against priestly concubinage to the indictment of lay investiture, from which all these abuses sprang. Gregory VII went even further by claiming freedom (*libertas*) for the Church, that is, independence from the emperor and the exclusive right to judge christian society.

Until recently there has been little interest in the spirituality of the gregorian reform, which historians have too often reduced to a mere movement of reaction against the abuses of feudalism in the ecclesiastical sphere. The meaning of that struggle, whose outcome was to be decisive for the Church, can, however, be understood only if it is placed in an eschatological perspective. The explanation for Gregory VII's epistolary violence, for the relentlessness with which he fought his foes—be they dissident bishops or the german emperor—does not only lie in the pontiff's passionate character. Gregory was convinced that the society of his time was a combat zone in which the disciples of Christ must wage a decisive battle against the forces of evil which were besieging the Church itself. In order to fulfil the supernatural mission assigned to it by its founder, the Church had to free itself from their grip, by violence if need be. Thus, in the minds of the Gregorians, a palpable distortion occurred on the eschatological plane: anxious expectation of the final catastrophe gave way to a desire to build the kingdom of God here and now. Since the end of time did not appear to be imminent, the Church could no longer be content with fostering the growth of the inner man in every Christian, while leaving it up to monarchs and princes to rule society as they pleased. It was now its responsibility to bring the entire universe to acknowledge the kingship of Christ, by embodying itself in visible structures and by resorting, if necessary, to power. It would thus be possible to build an earthly spiritual city. What medieval authors called the holy christian republic (*sancta res publica christiana*), we call christendom.

The will to act directly on the world in order to bring it into conformity with the divine will was already present in some bishops and abbots early in the eleventh century. When they took over the organization of the peace movements, thus substituting for the failure of royal authority, they started a process which was to lead the Church to intervene more and more frequently in secular affairs. This, indeed, had been correctly grasped by an imperial prelate, Bishop Gerard of Cambrai, who in 1033 had strenuously opposed the holding of peace assemblies in his diocese: in his view, guaranteeing public order was up to the king, not to the Church, and religious were overstepping their responsibility by becoming involved in temporal matters. From the clerics' earliest action in favor of peace to their deposing Henry IV, there is indeed a continuity and an indication of what medieval theocracy was to be: an attempt at building the kingdom of God here below. However, Gregory VII went further in that direction than the monks most open to the demands of the society of their day had ever done. Whereas Cluny, for instance, saw salvation only in the monastic institution and favored the contemplative life, the reforming pope launched a call to all Christians to act to reform both the Church and society. Praying for the world was no longer enough to save it; it was necessary to lead it. In the long run, monastic life was to emerge devalued from this transformation of spirituality, whereas the struggle for the faith and for the service of one's neighbor were to become the Christian's specific tasks. It is doubtless not by chance that the break between Rome and Constantinople was consummated in 1054, at the very time when, under the influence of the reform movement, the papacy and the western Church were embarking on entirely new paths in the religious sphere.

The gregorian reform coïncided approximately with the rise of feudalism in most western countries. With regard to the new nobility whose basic role and occupation was warfare, the Church took a cautious attitude for some time. Traditionally attached as it was to royal authority, it at first viewed the knights (*milites*) as no more than instigators of anarchy and disturbances. In the tenth century, for instance, the early Cluniacs virulently condemned the lay aristocracy's pride and the oppression to which it subjected the poor. As late as 950, Odo of Cluny abounded in invective against evil nobles who abused their power instead of putting it at the service of the common good. In extolling the figure of Saint Gerard of Aurillac, he highlighted the refusal to shed blood which set this pious layman off from his aristocratic circle. The Church severely condemned violence and warfare. Killing an enemy in battle, whatever the mitigating circumstances, was in its eyes a sin that defiled whoever committed it. But as early as this time attempts were made to christianize the knightly class (*militia*) through a process of sacralization to which the liturgy bears witness. In the Romano-Germanic Pontifical, a liturgical ritual drawn up in Mainz towards the middle of the tenth century, we find a ceremonial for the blessing of lances and swords, as well as a prayer over combatants. The rite of dubbing appeared in the eleventh century; until that time it had been an exclusively secular ceremony, but its religious character constantly asserted itself, finally to prevail in the thirteenth century. This new-found concern for the knights was not disinterested. His coronation empowered the carolingian king to defend the Church and even conferred on him the duty of doing so. In the new feudal context, the obligation went over to the masters of the soil and to the holders of public authority, that is, to the lords. By having himself dubbed according to a liturgical ceremonial, the knight (*miles*) committed himself to behaving as a soldier of Christ. Knighthood became the christian form of the military state.

This doubtless did not imply that the Church in any way approved of the violence arbitrarily perpetrated by the lords against one another and against unarmed people. In areas where territorial breakdown and the decay of political power were most advanced—from Poitou to Languedoc and Burgundy—, clerics were even seen to intervene directly to combat anarchy. But the Peace of God, for which gatherings such as those of Charroux and Narbonne attempted to win acceptance around the year 1000, did not forbid private wars; it simply condemned acts of violence against unarmed people and sacred places. Moreover, the Church strove to make the knights (*milites*) as close partners as possible in the decisions taken, which could not be enforced without their agreement and cooperation. Thus the peace to which the clerics had wished to give an inviolable and sacred stamp by means of oaths over relics often appeared as 'an expression of legalized violence, since establishing and defending it was the responsibility of those very persons who alone had the power really to stand in its way.'[17] After 1020, the promulgation of the Truce of God seemed to mark a turning point in the Church's attitude toward warfare. By restricting fighting in time, it appeared to discredit warlike acts themselves, holding them up as defiling in the same way as lust or the passion for gain. But the clerics' attitude toward violence remained ambiguous. First of all, they themselves did not hesitate to resort to arms in certain areas to repress violations of the law: in Poitou, peace armies formed under the supervision of monks and their vassals; in Bourges, in 1038, the archbishop organized a militia which launched attacks on the castles of mischief-making lords. These attempts were short-lived, but they witness to the appearance of a new mindset among churchmen, some of whom came to believe that the use of force was justified when, under their leadership, it was put to ends beneficial to christian society. Moreover, setting the number of days on which warfare was prohibited amounted in

---

[17]R. Fossier, 'Remarques sur l'étude des "commotions" sociales aux XIe et XIIe siècles', *Cahiers de Civilisation médiévale* 16 (1973) 45-50.

fact to acknowledging that it was permissible, if not legitimate, the rest of the time.

The struggle against Islam, especially in Spain, was to accelerate the shift toward an increasingly understanding attitude regarding the use of arms. In a letter addressed to the archbishop of Narbonne in 1063, Pope Alexander II— who in fact was drawing his inspiration from eleventh-century texts concerning the defence of Italy against the Saracens— stated that shedding the blood of infidels was not a sin. The document's great novelty resides in the pontiff's assertion that participation in a war useful to the Church constituted a penitential satisfaction, in the same way as almsgiving or pilgrimage. The frankish knights whom Cluny was then sending off in great numbers to fight the Moors at Toledo thus enjoyed the remission of the penalties inflicted on them for their sins, by virtue of this commutation of a rather original kind. Moreover, the popes of the gregorian period intervened on several occasions in battles which seemed important to them in order to mark the interest they took in the victory of one of the opposing sides. This favor was marked by the bestowal of the standard of Saint Peter (*Vexillum Sancti Petri*), an emblem which conferred a sacred character on the cause of the laymen who benefited from it, and endowed their wars with the appearance of a struggle for the faith. This occurred for instance in 1066, when Alexander II encouraged William the Conqueror to invade England; a few years earlier, Erlembaldo, leader of the Patarines of Milan, had seen his violent action against the simoniacal clergy and its defenders similarly ratified by the Church of Rome. This was a clearly gregorian initiative, in that it implied that the laity's stormy vocation to armed combat must remain within the limits of obedient support for the decisions of a reforming papacy. Gregory VII himself summoned kings to the defence of his cause, and as these kings betrayed him, called on great lords or ordinary faithful to put their swords at the service of the Apostolic See.

At the end of the eleventh century, the spirituality of the crusade grew out of the merger of all these elements. We must take good care not to forget that it was on the occasion of a peace assembly gathered at Clermont in 1095 that Pope Urban II launched the appeal which caused numberless faithful to leave for the Holy Land. To make the Peace of God prevail everywhere and free the Christians of the East from turkish oppression, it was necessary to do battle with the sword. The direct appeal launched by the papacy to the knights, bypassing the monarchs—at least at first—aroused a powerful movement in favor of the liberation of Christ's tomb. At the same time, it endowed the use of arms, which was the specific task of the feudal class, with the character of a religious act by making it the instrument of a christian restoration and of the propagation of the faith. With the advent of the crusades, fighting infidels, and later heretics and other enemies of the Church, became the new duty (*officium*) of the laity (*ordo laicorum*). The Clermont appeal offered the lay aristocracy a chance of ensuring its salvation without giving up its military vocation.

Bringing out the main themes of spiritual life in the West during the early feudal age is no easy undertaking. Situations vary from country to country, if not from region to region; thus, general statements are conjectural and unreliable. Moreover, even when we seem to grasp them, the realities of that time appear shifting and rife with contradictions. A few observations do, however, emerge as obvious. First, the massive supremacy of monastic spirituality which, beyond the world of the religious, exerted a deep influence on christian society as a whole. It was a spirituality of 'apartness', of rejection of—if not contempt for—the world, of eschatological anticipation. It is striking to realize that when, around the year 1000, lay people began to attain a more conscious religious life, they sought to live like monks or in their wake. Far from claiming any autonomy for the temporal sphere, they displayed a thirst for asceticism and an exaggerated spiritualism which led the most exacting of them to the brink of heresy. It is as though the faithful had wished to appropriate monasticism's religious ideal and observances in order to enjoy in return the graces and rewards promised to those who had given up the pleasures of life here below. The fascination exerted on lay people by such a demanding religious ideal appears surprising at first sight. However, the sharp contrasts between God and Satan, Good and Evil, spirit and flesh, conveyed by monastic spirituality, the place it afforded spiritual combat and the expectation of a better world, all very aptly answered the aspirations of simple, down-to-earth people, used to a hard life, for whom the Gospel had the flavor of novelty. The blend which then occurred between the monastic ideal and christian perfection was to leave a lasting mark on the notions which the common mentality harbored concerning sanctity. Until the thirteenth century at least, the faithful would spontaneously regard as a saint any man or woman who gave up worldly life in order to lead an austere existence and break his or her body through voluntary suffering.

The results of the gregorian reform were contradictory: by desacralizing temporal authority and extolling the priesthood, it increased the distance between clerics and laity. This separation was embodied in the organization of space inside churches: the twelth century witnessed the appearance of the choir screen or *jube*, a huge stone barrier adorned with carvings, which isolated the clerics, gathered together in the choir, from the faithful assembled in the nave. The former, with whom the Church increasingly tended to identify, claimed a monopoly of the sacred, whereas the latter were confined to secular activities. But lay people amply recovered in the spiritual sphere what the evolution of ecclesiology had deprived them of. A world which had become the stage of a decisive confrontation between the two Cities and the place where the kingdom of God was being built offered the faithful, and especially warriors, broad scope for action. By endowing warlike action with an active role in the life of the Church, the notion of the crusade as a work of God (*opus Dei*) presented the knightly class with a means of participating directly in the graces of salvation without having to give up its own state and values. In our twentieth-century eyes, slaying infidels or imposing baptism on vanquished peoples by force (a rather rare occurrence, in fact) may appear to be a strange form of christian life. But from the viewpoint of a history of medieval spirituality, the crusades are of interest to us less for their historical development than for their witness to the appearance of a new religious spirit. Indeed, behind the aristocracy, which, thanks to them, discovered a specific way of belonging to the Church, the mass of the poor and unarmed emerged. Many of them yearned for an authentic religious life and refused to let themselves be confined to a purely passive or instrumental role. This tension between the demands of a popular evangelism kindled by the gregorian reform and the attitude of the clerics whose tendency it was to make the sacred their province gave rise, in the twelfth century, to spiritual problems and movements of a new kind.

III

THE RELIGION
OF A NEW ERA

From the Late Eleventh to
the Early Thirteenth Century

THE NEW CONDITIONS OF SPIRITUAL LIFE

HISTORIANS OF THE MIDDLE AGES now agree that, in most areas of the West, the period extending from the late eleventh to the early thirteenth centuries (approximately between 1080 and 1220) was marked by a spectacular leap forward in all fields. It was, in Duby's words, 'the century of the great advance', marked both by unprecedented population growth and by the spread of new techniques which resulted in the rapid expansion of agricultural and industrial production. In a world which remained basically rural, the cities nonetheless experienced a genuine revival and new social groups made their appearance. Among them were the burghers, a category still poorly defined in the twelfth century, characterized both by urban residence and by the exercise of professions implying the ownership of a financial or cultural capital: merchants, shipowners, lawyers, notaries, and others. After centuries of resistance to change and of withdrawal into its shell, the West, beginning with Italy and the areas between the Seine and Escault rivers, was the stage of a genuine 'commercial revolution' (Robert S. Lopez) not entirely unlike the nineteenth-century industrial revolution. In any case, just like the latter, it produced changes

75

and upheavals whose repercussions quickly made themselves felt in the field of spiritual life.

The new society which arose in the twelfth century continued to evolve within the framework of feudalism, and countries such as Germany even experienced at this time the process of decay of authority which, in more westerly regions, had been completed around the first third of the eleventh century. Yet the feudal system, founded on the appropriation of power by the masters of the soil, was forced to adapt to the new conditions of economic life. The alluring prospects offered peasants by the pioneer fronts of settlement, as well as the increased mobility of manpower, compelled the lords to grant their tenants increased freedom, if not freedom pure and simple. In the cities, the arbitrary nature of the seignorial regime met with opposition from the most dynamic social groups. Within the framework of the communal movement, the burghers gradually wrested guarantees for the free exercise of their activities, and sometimes even urban autonomy, from the traditional holders of authority—counts or bishops.

The emergence of a profit mentality was perhaps the most important consequence of all these changes. The peasant who sought to increase his production or his livestock in order to earn a few farthings at market, the lord who had land cleared so as to add to the number of his men and to the rents he raised from them, the merchant who set out on land or sea with his bundles of cloth, were all motivated by the desire to earn money, and still more money. The clergy were not spared by this trend; C. Violante has aptly shown, in the case of Italy, how in the twelfth century the bishops managed to turn the economic expansion then taking place to good account.[1] Moreover, the growing wealth of monks is a common theme

---

[1]C. Violante, 'I vescovi dell'Italia centro-settentrionale e lo sviluppo dell'economia monetaria', in *Studi sulla cristianità medioevale* (Milan, 1972) 325–347.

in the literature of the period. The great abbeys had been the main beneficiaries of the return of tithes and churches by the laity under the influence of the gregorian reform. They may have found themselves short of funds at times, owing to poor management of their estates or to inordinate building expenses; their material prosperity was nonetheless obvious in the eyes of their contemporaries. At all levels of society, and especially in the cities, money took on growing importance in human relations and in daily life. Confronted with this new world, monastic theology and spirituality quickly revealed themselves unsuited. Many religious, accustomed to a stable and austere world, reacted with invective. In 1128, Abbot Rupert of Deutz presented the rise of the cities as a consequence of sin. In his view, towns were no more than dens of vile traffickers and disreputable charlatans. A few years earlier, one of his colleagues, Guibert of Nogent, had cast a final condemnation on the communal movement, which he had seen at work at Laon. This attitude of fear and rejection with regard to urban society subsided in time, but there were to be many clashes and conflicts before traditional spirituality adjusted to the new conditions of social life.

The economic expansion which the West experienced in the eleventh century had many consequences, not all of them beneficial. While it wrested society from stagnation, it increased the distance which separated rich from poor. Even within the peasantry, which until then had formed a more or less undifferentiated mass characterized by precarious conditions and a poor living standard, cleavages appeared between those who owned farming equipment—the husbandmen—, and the laborers, who had only their arms with which to work. Poverty, which until then had been experienced rather as a state of weakness—to be poor was to be defenceless before the mighty—, tended to become primarily a depressed economic condition and a mark of social decline. Whether for want of weapons in the knight's case, of books in the cleric's, or of a plow in the rustic's, the poor man was someone who lacked the means of maintaining his rank.[2] In the traditional rural society where everyone knew everyone else, he was certain to benefit from the solidarity of the group to which he belonged. Once the general use of money had relaxed such bonds and an urban environment had formed—one in which some degree of anonymity prevailed—, paupers became downgraded individuals, doomed to wandering or emigration. Their growing numbers and the fact that their destitution was more visible in the city than in the country did not fail to confront the consciences of Christians with new questions.

Finally, this new society was marked by increased mobility. Lords setting out on crusade, peasants going off to areas of settlement, clerics in search of schools and teachers, bishops or abbots on their way to Rome or to councils—all circles seemed agitated at the time by a thirst for travel and a change of scene. The inhabitants of the West, who with the exception of a small elite had long been confined to the horizon of their villages, no longer hesitated to embark on far-off expeditions which nonetheless remained perilous. The passion for pilgrimages, and especially for that of Santiago de Compostella, was but one expression of this travel fever which contrasted with the monastic ideal of stability and finally called it into question. In this new climate, outside influences made themselves more and more clearly felt in the area of spirituality. Eremitic experiments taking place in Calabria were soon heard of even in northern regions, as can be seen from the life of Saint Bruno at the turn of the eleventh century. Through italian merchants who were in contact with slavic lands, and perhaps through crusaders who had dwelt in the East, religious currents inspired by dualism entered the West during the second third of the twelfth century. Information and ideas were exchanged in mills and taverns, at markets

[2]M. Mollat, ' 'Le problème de la pauvreté au XIIe siècle', in *Vaudois languedociens et pauvres catholiques*, Cahiers de Fanjeaux, 2 (Toulouse, 1967) 23–47.

and at fairs. Learned controversies quickly found an echo in the public square: 'Discussions on the Holy Trinity spring up even at crossroads', as the bishops of the province of Sens wrote the pope in 1140; they anxiously saw the world of the schools joining up with that of the working people. Difficult communications notwithstanding, spiritual movements spread at an ever quicker pace, so greatly had the masses' receptivity increased. Another change was affecting the mental universe of the thirteenth century: a process of desacralization as regards the world. Sparked off by the gregorian reform, this led in the long run to the emancipation of lay society. In the twelfth century, this was still a distant prospect, and the Church's grip on society was perhaps never as powerful as in the time of Alexander III and Innocent III. But the influence of the movement was already beginning to make itself felt, driving clerics to question the relationship between the temporal and the spiritual. By desacralizing the Empire and lay investiture, Gregory VII and Yvo of Chartres worked unknowingly towards the formation of an autonomous secular society. By establishing a distinction between sacrament and sacramental, the latter put an end, at least at the conceptual level, to a confusion that had prevailed since carolingian times, and contributed to extricating the christian notion of the sacred from the sphere of magic.

On the theological plane, ideas were moving in the same direction. Between 1120 and 1140, the teachers of the school of Chartres reflected on the meaning of creation. They developed the notion that, far from dwelling in matter, God, after creating it, had withdrawn from it, leaving it up to humankind to subdue the universe. In such a perspective, seeking to know his will and the order in which he wished to maintain things seemed by no means an affront to his majesty. Creation was no longer regarded as a formless, mysterious jumble, but, in the famous words of Bernard of Chartres, as 'an ordered collection of creatures'. Far from being merely a debased reflection of the heavenly spheres, the universe possessed a reality of its own, which could become an object of study and interpretation. It was the end of the enchanted world. Of course, such notions long remained the province of a cultured elite, and even in clerical circles they were violently opposed by those who, like Saint Bernard, viewed the work of those theologians who strove to grasp divine mysteries solely with the resources of the intellect as a profanation and a sign of presumption. But when, in 1215, the Fourth Lateran Council decided that the Church would no longer credit ordeals with any value and that clerics were not to resort to them, it simply drew the conclusions of a movement which for the past century had been tending to establish, in Father Chenu's felicitous expression, 'a new balance between nature and grace'.[3]

Moreover, at least for some of its inhabitants, the world ceased to be the valley of tears of which monastic authors spoke. Economic growth, uneven from one area to the next but nonetheless real, the rise in living standards which was expressed within the aristocracy by a search for comfort and luxury, and finally the movement which led city and country dwellers towards freedom, all combined to make human life and worldly possessions less precarious and more attractive. The twelfth-century West was doubtless still far from being a society of abundance, and terrible famines, such as that of the years 1194-1199, continued to shake it periodically. Yet the world appeared more beautiful and more engaging— and not only to troubadours. The nobility, which enjoyed some leisure and was not yet impoverished, was able to rise to the pleasures of the mind and of culture; in the feudal courts of northern France, epic poems (*chansons de geste*) were composed, extolling the feats of warriors against a background of heroic Christianity. In the more secular courts of the South, men vied with each other in subtlety with a view to gaining the ladies' favors. Amorous strategy and casuistry were the

[3]M.-D. Chenu, 'Moines, clercs et laïcs au carrefour de la vie évangélique (XIIe s.)', *Revue d'Histoire ecclésiastique* 49 (1954) 59–89.

source of courtly poetry in which love became the subject matter *par excellence* of the entertainment which this refined society afforded itself. Though by no means platonic—it did not rule out carnal possession—, courtly love offers a good illustration of the distance man had assumed with respect to desire. But passion was no mere transposition of divine love; it was a basically new reality in which human love was self-sufficient and governed by its own logic. On the spiritual plane, the rise of a secular society and culture was to set off a twofold reaction: some, judging that these new attractions made the world more fearsome, met it with total rejection and withdrew to the desert. Others, having come to terms with the changes in progress, considered that resistance to evil did not necessarily entail escape from the world.

RETURN TO THE SOURCES:
APOSTOLIC LIFE AND GOSPEL LIFE

As early as the middle of the eleventh century, the demand for a deeper religious life surfaced almost everywhere in the West. It occurred first in Italy because of its proximity of the byzantine world, from which intense spiritual incitements radiated. Starting with the 1080s, the movement spread to northwestern Europe, where it bore its finest fruits. This longing to live one's faith better, of which historians take note without being able to provide a good explanation for it, expressed itself primarily by a will to return to the sources, which was in fact one of the outstanding trends of the cultural life of the period. For twelfth-century people, conscious as they were of being the unworthy heirs of a brilliant past, progress lay in the rediscovery of a tradition which had been lost sight of because of the harshness of the times. This fascination exercised by origins was marked, in the field of literary expression, by a concern with drawing one's inspiration from good latinity, Cicero's and Virgil's rather than Macrobius' or Lactantius'. In Bologna, Irnerius and the glossators returned roman law to its place of honor. Its texts were gradually pieced back together in their entirety; incomplete collections and compilations contaminated by the influence of barbarian law were eliminated. In every field of intellectual life, the twelfth century appealed to a more authentic tradition against impure traditions.

The Church did not remain aloof from this back-to-the-sources movement. For it as well, perfection was to be found in the past, that is, in the time of the apostles and martyrs. In the eyes of many clerics, the world could only grow old and decline as that blessed era receded. The eleventh-century reformers are to be credited with believing and proving by example that the Church would be restored to fresh youth by drawing its inspiration from that past, which, often in its history, acted as a dynamic and stimulating myth. Gregory VII aptly expressed this new mindset when he wrote: 'The Lord did not say: my name is custom, but: my name is Truth'. Hence his refusal to acknowledge the validity of practices which had crept into the clerical world over the centuries in the name of fidelity to authentic Tradition, of which the Church of Rome was the sole guarantor and interpreter. During the same period, hermits were seen to desert monastic communities in large numbers in order to rediscover the way of life long ago practised by the Desert Fathers. A little later, the Cistercians broke with Cluny in the name of a return to the Rule of Saint Benedict, which had been obscured and warped by observances based on custom. In brief, all the religious experiments of that time were marked by a will to revert to the original purity of Christianity. The ideal of the early Church model (*Ecclesiae primitivae forma*) became the necessary reference of the new spirituality which, by an apparent paradox, sought the answer to the problems raised by a changing society in increased fidelity to the witness of the apostles and to the message of the Gospel.

In practice, this longing to revive the perfection of the early Church expressed itself in the ideal of apostolic life (*vita apostolica*). The notion that the primitive community of Jerusalem as depicted in the Acts of the Apostles[4] was a model for the Church and that its way of life was the very type of the perfect life found an echo in all circles. These texts had, of course, aroused interest before the eleventh century. But they had been monopolized by the monks, who throughout the early Middle Ages had put themselves forward as the apostles' authentic successors and imitators. Were they not leading the apostolic life, since, having renounced both personal possessions and self-will, they lived together to serve the Lord better?[5] In fact, until the middle of the eleventh century, no one questioned the idea that christian perfection was achieved in the cloister. We can begin to detect a reaction against such notions with the advent of the gregorian reform. Gregory VII himself, when he was still only Archdeacon Hildebrand, attempted to extend to the entire clergy the benefit of the common life, which was central to the apostolic ideal. He failed in this undertaking, and the roman synod of 1059 merely advised priests to 'hold in common all that accrued to them from the Church'. At this level, the apostolic life appeared as a means to the moral and disciplinary reform of the clergy. By striving to have clerics live in community, the papacy was particularly aiming at removing them from the authority of lay lords so as to place them under the bishops' control. This was still asking too much, and those who complied with such instructions were a minority. They took the name regular canons, as opposed to the secular canons who, refusing the discipline of the common dormitory and refectory, retained their personal possessions as the Acts of The Synod of Aachen (816) allowed them to do.

[4]Ac 2:44: 'The faithful all lived together and owned everything in common,' and 4:32: 'The whole group of believers was united, heart and soul. No one claimed for his own use anything that he had, as everything they owned was held in common.'
[5]M.-H. Vicaire, *L'imitation des apôtres: moines, chanoines et mendiants (IVe-XIIIe siècle)* (Paris:1963).

The gregorian notion of the apostolic life, which most clergy found too exacting, conversely appeared inadequate to some minds enamored of perfection. Among regular canons and hermits, many, not content with imitating monastic observances, went so far as to assert that clerics were the true successors of the apostles. Indeed, monasticism, by eliminating confrontation with the world through enclosure, had reduced the apostolate to personal sanctification, whereas a careful re-reading of Acts brought out how important a part of the apostles' vocation the ministry of preaching and of announcing the Gospel had been.[6] In a world which was less to be escaped than to be conquered and saved, the care of souls (*cura animarum*), which monks did not generally exercise, tended to become one of the essential elements of the apostolic life. Thus following the model of the early Church meant not simply living in community and without private property, but reaching out to others. Such opening up to the outside world took very different forms according to circumstances, from the development of hospitality and charity to the ministry of preaching.

We must relate this deepening of the religious ideal to the transformations undergone by piety. Were we to define the 'ages of the world' by their essential religious features, as medieval authors did, we might say that the period reaching from the late eleventh to the early thirteenth century was truly the age of Christ. Not that the spirituality of the early Middle Ages and of feudal monasticism had underestimated the figure of the Saviour: already Alcuin, and later the great abbots of Cluny, had shown deep veneration for the Cross. Generally speaking, however, before the twelfth century Christ was viewed especially as the second person of the Trinity and as the fearsome Judge who was to return at the end of time. That is, in fact, the image conveyed to us by the tympanums

[6] Ac 4:33: 'The apostles continued to testify to the resurrection of the Lord Jesus with great power'.

of many romanesque churches. The evidence of art, like that of spiritual literature, confirms that the minds of that time were more sensitive to the divine transcendance than to the Incarnation, and to the Transfiguration than to the Passion. As early as the mid-eleventh century, a great monastic theologian, Saint Anselm, sparked off a decisive turn in the religious evolution of the Middle Ages by asking in one of his treatises the basic question: *Cur Deus homo?* Why did God become man? He answered it by showing that the salvation of humankind absolutely required that God become incarnate and share the human condition. Even though Saint Anselm was not understood in his lifetime, he emerged as the fore-runner of the twelfth century's great spiritual orientations in stressing the infinite love of the Word made flesh and the greatness of the Virgin Mary. Let us make no mistake, however: the hour of tender or moving devotion to the humanity of Christ had not yet come, even though some signs already heralded it, as we see in the treatise by the Cistercian Aelred of Rievaulx entitled *When Jesus was twelve years old*. The God-man extolled in the spirituality of the time was in fact the Christ of the Gospels. The new-found awareness of the Incarnation did not let itself be dissociated from the contemplation of the divine glory. Neither Autun nor Vézelay speak to us of the historical Jesus, nor of emotion. Like Saint Bernard, they present us with Christ the King, God the Saviour, Love personified.

The central place held by Christ in the piety of twelfth-century Christians was expressed, on the level of spirituality, by the greater value afforded the New Testament. A more exacting fidelity to the word of God led the best minds beyond a moral and disciplinary notion of the apostolic life. As early as the beginning of the twelfth century, many fervent communities referred less to the text of the Acts of the Apostles than to the Gospel passages which could provide rules of life, especially those where the poverty of Christ and his disciples is mentioned. Stephen of Muret (d.1124), founder of the order of Grandmont, wrote significantly: 'The only rule of life is the Gospel; it is the rule of Jesus Christ, more perfect than that of Saint Benedict.' Likewise Saint Norbert, in creating the premonstratensian order, enjoined his disciples to 'follow the holy Scriptures and take Christ as their guide'. For those who adhered to the new spirituality, love of God was expressed by as faithful as possible an imitation of the life of the Lord. 'Following, naked, the naked Christ' (*nudus nudum Christum sequi*)[7] and evangelizing the poor were the two basic requirements laid down by twelfth-century spiritual movements.

The will to model oneself on the Christ of the Gospels was expressed first of all by added demands in the field of poverty. By stressing communal ownership, the *vita apostolica* abolished the distinction between rich and poor. It was practised by monks and regular canons, who gave up individual ownership on entering religious life. But at the practical level, such communal aspirations could very well go along with the collective ownership of considerable possessions, as was the case with most abbeys and chapters. Those who wanted to follow the Gospel to the letter owed it to themselves to go further, that is, to live as 'Christ's poor', restricting themselves to the bare minimum, and sometimes to less than that. Stephen of Muret wished the Grandmontines' estates to be so small that they would be compelled to beg outside for part of their living. Though all the adherents of the genuinely apostolic life (*vita vere apostolica*) did not go as far, austerity and material poverty were nonetheless the major concerns of the groups who claimed that ideal as their own.

An example may show us to what practical attitudes the new spirituality could lead. In 1083, six robber barons who had been converted by a monk settled in a solitary spot in Brabant

---

[7]As R. Grégoire has shown in a recent study, 'L'adage ascétique *Nudus nudum Christum sequi*', *Studi Storici in onore di O. Bertolini* (Pisa, 1972) 1:395–409, this is a traditional expression which dates back to Saint Jerome, but it is in the twelfth century that it appears frequently in texts, where it marks the desire to live in total poverty.

called Afflighem in order to dedicate themselves to religious life together.[8] The very choice of the place was significant: it was an uncultivated and uninhabited zone, but was located near the road from Bruges to Cologne, a route much travelled by pilgrims and merchants. Until then the area had been a bandits' haunt; the new monks made it secure and provided hospitality for wayfarers. The community had the count of Louvain guarantee it the right of freely electing its abbot, and the local bishop exempted it from all rents. It was decided that the tithes on all revenues were to be set aside for the poor. Moreover, the founders devoted the best part of their efforts and resources to building and enlarging the hospice, which soon came to include two buildings. For their own use the monks put up a modest oratory, and for a long time they were content with a mere shed. The community's survival was ensured partly by the cultivation of its land, but also by manual work and the alms of the faithful. Thus the very structure of its income expressed a spirit of abandonment to Providence well in keeping with the founders' evangelism. The same inspiration is evidenced by the monks' concern to avoid any infringement on the possessions of others, as well as in their refusal to bring lawsuits against those who wronged them or to accept certain donations, such as churches, deemed incompatible with their ideal. The new foundation met with rapid success: converts, both clerics and lay people, soon flocked to Afflighem, whole families at a time. After some initial trial and error, all finally found their place in the community: the monks in choir, the laybrothers in the fields, and the women in priories of nuns that spread into the surrounding countryside. In this specific case, the experience took place within a monastic framework, that of the benedictine rule. But one could quote a great many foundations of that period

[8]Ch. Dereine, 'La spiritualité "apostolique" des premiers fondateurs d'Afflighem (1085–1100)', *Revue d'Histoire ecclésiastique* 54 (1959) 41–65.

which were initially impelled by the same spirit but ended up with different institutional structures. Indeed, rather than a moral agenda or a well-defined way of life, the apostolic ideal may be defined as a mindset which could find expression in many different fashions.

TRANSFORMATIONS IN RELIGIOUS LIFE

During the early Middle Ages and the early feudal age, monastic life had been the only expression of the ideal of christian perfection, aside from a few isolated eremitical experiences. Such monolithism was well suited to a static society characterized by spiritual and cultural lifelessness. But as the West awakened and as its structures became more complex, the aspirations of the faithful could no longer be satisfied within the single framework of traditional monasticism. Next to it, itself called on to undergo reform, new forms of consecrated life based on original spiritualities arose and developed. Although by definition they were outside the world, even religious in some way reflected the tensions and contradictions of the society around them.

These various movements had in common a demand for authenticity and for a personalization of religious life. Practices which had been accepted for centuries were suddenly questioned in the name of fidelity to the Gospel. Within monasticism itself, and even more so outside it, the virtues of ritualism were challenged. In the abbeys of the early feudal age, most of the monks were oblates, that is, children entrusted to the monastery by their parents at a very young age. Indeed, the 'work of God' (*Opus Dei*) was viewed as an activity for which no special vocation was needed. Offering one's son as a monk was no more a problem than was sending him off to another lord as a squire to learn to bear arms: a worker was required, not to like his job, but to do it conscientiously. The monk who recited the office correctly and in its entirety was doing his duty, even if his heart was not always in it. Moreover, the individual existed solely with reference to the group, and the psalmody of each religious was of value only insofar as it blended into the liturgical chanting of a community. One might almost say that concern for the outer perfection and splendor of worship could become an obstacle to the personal deepening of faith. Thus, in most of the religious movements which appeared at the dawn of the twelfth century, we find a longing to shake off the yoke of routine in order to allow individuals to enlist freely and personally in the service of Christ. The new orders admitted only adults, regardless of whether their entry into religious life was the result of a vocation which had been maturing since their youth or whether it had required a break with worldly life, that is, a conversion.

Moreover, a more refined sense of things religious, not unrelated to the progress of education, made many Christians more sensitive to the discrepancies existing between the visible aspect of the Church and the ideal which should have inspired it. Such a requirement for compliance with the Gospel model had already manifested itself in the eleventh century in the field of morals. In many parts of christendom, the faithful, wanting their priests to lead chaste lives, had sometimes even forced them to practise celibacy, which in their eyes would guarantee the effectiveness of their sacramental ministry. In the twelfth century, criticism shifted from the clergy's mores to its wealth and power. The most exacting minds were scandalized at seeing abbeys and cathedral chapters ensconced in both feudal society and the seigniorial system. For the tenth and eleventh-century reforms had, in many cases, allowed for the restoration and even the growth of ecclesiastical estates; the great reforming abbots were usually also good administrators, concerned with stabilizing and reinforcing the material foundations of religious life so as to ensure regular observance and to give divine worship greater brilliance. The result was that although the monks remained individually poor, they became collectively rich: 'A knight becomes a monk, but goes from poverty to riches' (*Fit monachus miles, sed fit de paupere dives*), as a canon in western France noted around 1080 concerning nobles who took the monastic habit.[9] Moreover, the religious devoted more and more of their time to the management of their possessions, as well as to lawsuits against heirs who showed no eagerness to execute the wills made by their parents in favor of the churches. Even the scattering of real estate bequeathed by the laity, which usually consisted in small plots as well as in tithes, altars, and portions of churches, entailed serious disadvantages for cenobites. Many of them were sent to live alone or in pairs in faraway priories in order to supervise the tilling of the land. The result was a noticeable slackening in observance and often a contamination of the monks by the society around them. The splendor of the liturgy in the great abbeys like Cluny or Saint-Denis did not make up for this *de facto* secularization of monasticism, of which growing wealth was only one aspect. Faced with such an evolution of cenobitic life, many Christians in search of spiritual perfection preferred to experiment with new forms of religious life rather than enrol among the black monks.

Eremitism

Eremitism was no twelfth-century invention. Already in the early Middle Ages, we hear of men who had retreated deep into the woods to lead a solitary, wandering religious existence. In benedictine monasteries, the abbot could exceptionally allow a monk of tried and tested spiritual mettle to leave the community in order to dwell for some time in the 'desert'. On the whole, such solitaries were few in number and do not seem to have had much influence on their contemporaries. Conversely, beginning in the eleventh century, and continuing especially in the twelfth, eremitism became a widespread phenomenon which appeared as an alternative to monastic life.

[9]Quoted by Jean Leclercq, 'La crise du monachisme aux XIe et XIIe siècles', in *Aux sources de la spiritualité occidentale* (Paris, 1964) 179.

This rapid development of eremitism, which began in Italy around the year 1000 with Saint Romuald, the founder of Camaldoli, also sprang from a return to the sources. Byzantine influences reached the West through southern Italy, and in the christian East the tradition of the Desert Fathers—the solitary ascetics of the Thebaid—had remained alive. It regained all its prestige and its drawing force in the West in the wake of economic and social change. The earliest developments of the trade economy and of urban growth aroused a reaction of rejection in some circles, especially among aristocrats and townspeople. In a complete about-face quite typical of the medieval mentality, they burned what they had hitherto worshiped and passed from riches to extreme destitution, from social to anachoritic life. As Léopold Genicot has correctly pointed out, 'in the eleventh century, the cities were becoming large enough to turn away religious souls; they were not yet large enough to create spiritual problems serious enough to lead the best of them to dedicate themselves to an apostolate among the urban masses.'[10] Hermits were also drawn in large numbers from the secular clergy. In many areas, the latter resisted all reform; this led a number of its members to leave priestly communities or chapters of lukewarm fervor for the countryside, and especially for forests and moors, those favorite haunts of solitaries. In western France, in Limousin and in Lotharingia, clerical eremitism experienced a spectacular development during the early twelfth century, one made famous by the names of Robert of Arbrissel, Peter of Craon and Stephen of Obazine, to list only the greatest.

Twelfth-century eremitism was not identical to that of earlier periods. It too had felt the influence of the ideal of apostolic life, and its spirituality is marked by it. The hermits of the time were in fact penitents: they were always crudely dressed, and their appearance was neglected, if not ghastly.

---

[10]L. Genicot, 'L'érémitisme du XIe siècle dans son contexte économique et social', in *L'eremitismo in Occidente nei secoli XIe XII* (Milan, 1965) 69.

They searched out the most appalling places, sleeping in
caves on the bare ground or building themselves huts out
of branches. Their diet consisted of a few vegetables and
whatever food they could gather; it never included meat or
wine. Living alone as they did, unhelped by anyone, they had
to be doubly wary of the devil's temptations. Thus, in spite
of the asceticism to which they doomed themselves, hermits
led an active life, not a purely contemplative one as did the
recluses, those men and women who dwelt shut up in a cell
adjoining a church or monastery. Out of necessity and by
virtue of their vocation, they had to work with their hands;
finally, they wore beards and traveled on foot or mounted on
a donkey, never on horseback.

Though hermits had fled the world, they had not thereby
become indifferent to other people, and secular and hagiographic literature depicts them as lavishing advice and comfort
on those who sought them out. Their mobility and freedom
allowed them to exercise a very varied ministry, which might
include anything from aid to wayfarers to popular preaching,
as was the case with wandering preachers (*Wanderprediger*)
such as Robert of Arbrissel or Bernard of Tiron, who traveled
back and forth across western France in the early twelfth
century, followed by bands of faithful disciples carried away
by their words. Even Stephen of Muret, that most stable of
hermits, did not hesitate to state that, good though it was
to renounce the world, snatching souls from the devil was
better yet. These solitaries were therefore not solely concerned
with the salvation of their souls. They looked toward others,
especially toward the very poor.

In the eremitical experiences of the period, the individual
phase was often of short duration. Successful hermits normally
attracted disciples and frequently founded religious communities gathered around places of worship. Eremitism in those
days was more a mindset than a form of life. It may be defined
as cenobitism on a small scale, one quite free and rural, as
opposed to the disciplined, often urban cenobitism of the old
orders. It could lead just as well to crusading—in the case

of Peter the Hermit—as to the practice of hospitality or to monastic and canonical foundations of a new kind. By virtue of a personal choice on the part of the founder or under pressure from a bishop, the Rule of Saint Benedict was sometimes chosen (as at Savigny or La Chaise-Dieu), or sometimes that of Saint Augustine. But often foundations of eremitical origin adopted original constitutions. At Fontevrault, Robert of Arbrissel created a double monastery under the direction of an abbess. In Italy, Camaldoli and Vallombrosa strove to combine the demands of eremitism with those of cenobitism in establishments which included both a monastery where monks prayed and worked in common, and hermitages where religious lived in solitude and practised the harshest brand of asceticism—the bond between the two being ensured by the obligation of taking meals in common. As for the Grandmontines, they followed Stephen of Muret's instructions in championing uncompromising poverty, given material expression by restrictions imposed on collective property. They also singled themselves out by the fact that the laybrothers—that is, the non-clerical members—were afforded supremacy over the monks in the order's government.

The only eremitical foundation which, without ever mustering large numbers, nonetheless experienced lasting success and left a deep mark on the spirituality of the medieval West was the carthusian order. It arose at the end of the eleventh century under the impetus of Saint Bruno, the head of the school at Reims, who retreated with a few companions to the wild Chartreuse valley near Grenoble. From the beginning, the new community was characterized by a very strict life of penance and by the will to break completely with the outside world. Saint Bruno (d.1101) too sought to reconcile the demands of the eremitic ideal with the necessities of cenobitism. He retained, besides the vows of chastity and stability, the submission of the religious to the prior and the practice of fraternal correction in chapter. But the elements borrowed from benedictine monasticism were not central. In the *Customs* drawn up by Guigo the Elder, fifth prior of La

Grande-Chartreuse, and adopted by the whole order in the mid-twelfth century, the masterword is solitude. Shut up in his cell, which he did not even leave in order to take his meals, the religious was to read, pray and meditate in silence, far from all stir and bustle, in order to attain perfect humility and hear God's voice. But there was no angelism in this spirituality: the hermit monk provided for his own needs and worked with his hands, usually by copying texts. Moreover, the outside world was not ignored. The Carthusians gave alms, welcomed guests, and prayed for humankind. 'Christ's name is Jesus,' wrote Guigo; 'therefore, from the very moment you lose, for whatever reason, the will to save any person, you cut yourself off from the members of Christ.' The influence of eremitism was expressed by the search for union with God in contemplation. Conversely, the liturgy's place in the new order was a modest one; the Carthusians came together only for the night office and for some of the day hours. Although most of them were priests, they rarely celebrated Mass.

In spite of certain appeareances which liken them to monks, the Carthusians were thus in the exact line of contemporary eremitism, and they represent one of its most remarkable outcomes. Their spirituality was the result of a new, more individualistic mentality, oriented toward freer personal experiences and towards the acquisition of an intimate religious life. All hermits did not reach such summits: some sank into extravagance or madness; others drifted to the brink of heresy, as did a certain Engelbald of Hérival in Lorraine, who, judging himself unworthy of the Church's sacraments, refused to the end to build a place of worship, to celebrate Mass and to receive communion. Though such an attitude was doubtless extreme, it is not unrelated to the Carthusians' reserved stance as regards the liturgy and to Robert of Arbrissel's reluctance concerning the building of churches. Behind these somewhat unruly sproutings of eremitism, which scandalized the clergy of the day, a new concept of the christian life was emerging, one in which salvation no longer depended on human mediations or on the practice of observances, since every person could privately encounter the saving Christ in his or her innermost self.

Canonical life

In other cases, far from leading clerics to the 'desert', the yearning for perfection drove them to adopt a strictly communal life connected with the practice of poverty; this is referred to in the writings of the period as 'canonical life' (*vita canonica*) or 'apostolic life' (*vita apostolica*). Were priests to some extent not entitled to consider themselves invested with a specific religious mission, since, in the words of a canonical customary, they 'succeeded Christ and the apostles in preaching, baptism, and the other sacraments of the Church'?[11] Urban II acknowledged this officially in 1090 by asserting the apostolic nature of the canons' way of life, and by placing them on the same level as the monks. For the first time in centuries, the priesthood could again be regarded as a state of perfection.

We must hasten to state that this possibility was a theoretical one, since most clergy refused to submit to such an exacting ideal. Though common-life schemes met with outright success in Italy and Provence, in northern areas they came up against the hostility of a clergy which remained very much attached to carolingian structures. Closely bound to aristocratic circles by the private-church system, the canons of those parts would not hear of a reform which would have led them to give up their prebends. Thus in northern France and in the Rhineland, regular canons appeared on the scene instead as a result of individual 'conversions' of clerics who, out of fervor, abandoned the traditional institutions. They often founded new churches, both urban and rural, next to secular chapters and collegiate churches. Other communities took up

[11]*Coutumier de l'ordre de Saint-Ruf*, ed. A. Carrier de Belleuse (Sherbrooke, 1950) 97.

the canonical life after a more or less long-term eremitical experience. Such was, for instance, the case of Arrouaise[12] in Picardy, and especially of Prémontré, near Laon, founded by Saint Norbert in 1120.[13] Finally, in some cases, groups of penitents (for example, at L'Artige in Limousin) or of hospitallers (at Roncevaux or the Great Saint Bernard) adopted this form of life, which was better suited to their charitable activity than was the monastic state.

The world of regular canons was thus a very diversified one, and the foundations which adopted the canonical life (*vita canonica*) appear less as the end-point of a general reform of clergy than as religious orders of a new kind. Their spirituality is difficult to define, the more so since although, after much trial and error, all these communities adopted the Rule of Saint Augustine early in the twelfth century, they accorded it neither the same content nor the same significance. Most regular canons contented themselves with following the First Rule (*Regula prima*), actually a letter of Saint Augustine in which the bishop of Hippo described the daily life of the small priestly community gathered around him in a 'monastery of clerics'. The practices recommended by this text are moderate, and the emphasis is on the common life and the absence of private property. Those who lived by this rule made up the 'old observance' (*ordo antiquus*), especially well represented in mediterranean regions.

But many new foundations, especially those of eremitic origin, wished to go further. They preferred to take as their reference a text entitled *Monastery observance* (*Ordo monasterii*) or *Second Rule* (*Regula secunda*). The latter was attributed to Saint Augustine, although for the most part it was not authored by him. It was a very exacting rule of life, which

[12]Ludo Milis, *L'ordre des chanoines réguliers d'Arrouaise* (Bruges, 1969).

[13]Concerning this matter, see the valuable clarification by Jean Becquet, 'Chanoines réguliers et érémitisme clérical', *Revue d'Histoire de la Spiritualité* 48 (1972) 361–370.

emphasized asceticism (fasting, silence, simplicity in dress) as well as manual work and poverty. The canons who wished to practice this ideal of genuinely apostolic life (*vita vere apostolica*) formed the 'new observance' (*ordo novus*) which, despite its name, was not a new religious order but a rigoristic current within the world of regular canons. Those who joined it were especially numerous in the area between the Seine and Rhine rivers. The most perfect expression of their spiritual ideal is to be found in the rule of Prémontré, which, alone among these groups, achieved an influence that extended to the bounds of christendom.

In spite of the differences separating their various branches, the regular canons developed an original spirituality to which the Christians of the twelfth-century were responsive: in some parts of the West at the time, there were as many augustinian canons as monks, if not more. Those who adhered to the *ordo antiquus* offered the example of an often intense religious life, unfolding within an extremely flexible institutional framework. For the Rule of Saint Augustine is not the counterpart of Saint Benedict's; it lacks both the latter's precision and its mandatory character. At most, it defines a framework and a spiritual climate; adaptation to local conditions or to the founder's intentions was ensured by constitutions particular to each house or order. Moreover, the canons lived in close contact with the world, in small communities established in town[14] or country collegiate churches where, besides the ministry of worship, they took on social duties which might include anything from the education of children to the care of the sick. Not by chance would Saint Dominic, in the thirteenth century, explicitly insert his order of 'canon-preachers', close to the laity and open to its problems, 'into the classic patterns of the canonical tradition'.[15]

---

[14]Literally *castrum*, a walled town which was not a city. (Translator's note)

[15]M.-H. Vicaire, *L'imitation*, p. 80.

Moreover, the regular canons developed an original spirituality based on an exalted notion of the priesthood. For the canonical movement's objective was not, at the start, to monasticize the secular clergy. In the view of its supporters, the goal of community life, beyond the moral or disciplinary advantages it included, was first and foremost to contribute to building the Church. Within the *ordo novus* or 'new observance,' a rigorous notion of asceticism no doubt prevailed, but its aim was not restricted to individual perfection. Inasmuch as he was the necessary intermediary between God and men, the priest who offered the sacrifice of the altar for the faithful had to purify himself by separating himself from the world through life in the cloister and by giving an example of evangelical poverty. The observances of the canons of Arrouaise or of Prémontré may appear very similar to those of the monks of their time; they were, however, set off from them by their end, which was apostolic rather than eschatological. Study, which held a large place in the canons' life, prepared them not only to pray well, therefore, but to preach well. Likewise, the center of their daily life was not so much the recitation of the hours as the conventual Mass, since the priest's office was primarily to offer sacrifice.

In the course of the controversies which pitted them against the monks throughout the twelfth century, the regular canons were led to spell out the basic implications of their way of life. For the first time in the history of western spirituality, clerics rejected the absolute primacy of the contemplative life and emphasized the value of action, which they placed on the same level. To quote a Premonstratensian, Anselm of Havelberg,

> The son of God, model of the highest contemplation as of the most perfect action, offered an example of both lives in his one person, for the benefit of all Christians and more especially of his apostles... We must therefore believe that they organized their life in order that, blessed pure of heart that they were, they might see the God of gods through contemplation in Zion, while, as blessed merciful ones longing to receive mercy,

they took care of their neighbors by preaching, healing and spreading the Gospel.[16]

In actual fact, although the priestly ideal of the first generation—that of the founders—was still very much marked by the climate of the gregorian reform, with its pronounced emphasis on chastity and separation from the world, after 1130 many congregations of regular canons, such as the Premonstratensians, were seen to stress the care of souls (*cura animarum*), which was no longer restricted to liturgical service in churches, but extended to the ministry of charity and of the word. This was especially noticeable in the germanic world and in eastern Europe, where the regular canons, who were prominent as settlers of new lands, zealously took on parochial duties.

Canonical spirituality did not long succeed in preserving its specificity and impact, however. Inasmuch as it established a close bond between the priestly ideal and the practise of a community life which was impracticable for many liturgical ministers, it scarcely influenced the latter. Such a state of affairs was to have serious consequences: throughout the Middle Ages and even up to the Council of Trent, the ordinary priest had no spiritual models suited to his concrete situation and his cultural level. It is in fact significant that until Saint Yves of Brittany (d.1303) no country or city priest belonging to the secular clergy was ever considered a saint by the Church. Moreover, the regular canons' lifestyle rather quickly showed a tendency to approximate that of monks. Proof of this may be found in the spiritual treatise entitled *The Cloister of the Soul* (*De claustro animae*), written about 1160 by a canon named Hugh of Fouilly. It gives a purely defensive definition of religious life—the cloister is presented as a camp fortified against temptations—which one would have expected from a monastic author. All that eventually remained of the

[16]Ibid.

attempt to bring clerics to adopt the apostolic life was clerical celibacy—which would long remain more an ideal than a reality—and religious orders whose main merit was to have shown that material and spiritual concern for one's neighbor was an essential dimension of the consecrated life.

The new monasticism

Directly or indirectly called into question by most of the religious movements we have just mentioned, benedictine monasticism nevertheless experienced its greatest splendor between the late eleventh century and the first decades of the twelfth. The choir of the immense basilica of Cluny III was dedicated by Urban II in 1095, and that of Saint-Benoît-sur-Loire in 1108. But this very success gave rise to criticism in the spiritual circles where the ideal of the apostolic life was at work. They incriminated the black monks, and especially Cluny, not only for being wealthy and bogged down in temporal affairs, but also for having lost sight of the very spirit of early monasticism, which had been neither liturgical nor priestly, but penitential. Contrary to a widely held view, the monastic institution did not undergo a crisis at the end of the eleventh century, and the birth of Cîteaux was not brought about by the decadence of Cluny. Trouble did not in fact begin in the great burgundian abbey until the abbacy of Pons of Melgueil (1109-1122). His successor, Peter the Venerable, managed to redress the situation and restore the monastery to its full prestige. The Cistercians drew clear of Cluny, then at the height of its fervor, not because they condemned it but because they wanted something else. If tensions and cleavages did occur in the world of the cloister, they existed to the extent that a new spirituality was calling into question what had hitherto prevailed.

Indeed, with Robert of Molesme, founder of Cîteaux in 1098, its third abbot Stephen Harding, and Saint Bernard, who gave the new foundation a decisive impulse from 1112 onward, an original concept of religious life appeared. Like all the spiritual movements of the time, it was based on the will to return to the sources. Cîteaux did not claim to innovate; it reverted to tradition, that is, to the primitive rule of Saint Benedict which had been distorted by custom. Through the Rule applied in its full purity, the white monks would seek to imitate Christ by going back to evangelical simplicity and the practise of poverty. The emphasis was on bareness and austerity. The cenobite was primarily a penitent who had fled the world to weep for his sins. He was to take refuge in solitude and silence—like the hermits—and detach himself completely from the world, both through the uncompromising observance of enclosure and through ascetic exercises. Thus the Cistercians preferred to settle in 'deserts'—marshy valleys or forest clearings far from population centers—and refused to take on any kind of parochial ministry. This exacting ideal led the founders to set up an original economic organization: so as not to be compelled to the travel detrimental to the strictness of their observances or to community life, the white monks cultivated their lands themselves and accepted neither seigniorial revenues nor ecclesiastical benefices. 'We are to have no revenues' (*Quod redditus non habeamus*), says the Charter of Charity, that basic text which codifies the experience of the first cistercian generation. The estates, insofar as possible unbroken and located close to the monastery, were tilled by laybrothers who lived next to the professed monks. Thus the latter were not distracted from the community life within which each fulfilled his vocation.

This aspiration to poverty was expressed in practice by a poor lifestyle. The clothing adopted was white, that is, made of undyed woolen material. Food was simple and frugal: a single meal a day, no meat or fish, only bread and vegetables seasoned with salt and oil, not to mention the frequent fasts. The dormitories had no conveniences, and the monks slept fully dressed. Simplicity and bareness were also the rule in buildings: there were to be no decorations or esthetic refinements. In contrast to the black monks' magnificent structures, the churches had neither ornaments nor costly liturgical furnishings; no stained glass windows, no organ, a deliberate choice of bareness which allowed only the image of the Crucified in the conventual church. The obligation of actual manual labor was reinstated by the statutes, which are positive on this point: 'If the brethren are compelled by necessity or poverty to work in the harvest themselves, they shall not be distressed on that account. They are not truly monks unless they live by the work of their hands.'[17] On average, the cistercian monk worked from four to six hours a day in the fields; as an indirect consequence, the office was shortened and simplified: all liturgical practices not mentioned in the rule were abolished, except for daily Mass and the office of the dead. A new balance was thus established between the life of prayer, physical work, and meditative reading.

All these demands aimed at rediscovering not only the letter of the benedictine rule but its spirit. Indeed, the Cistercians were convinced that observing its basic prescriptions could lead to the perfection of charity even here below. They thereby shared the new religious mentality which sought to reduce the gap between ideal and lived reality, and considered the validity of witness to be dependent on the worthiness of the apostle. They also reflected the spirit of the times in that they received only adults into their monasteries and increased the time accorded for private prayer in the very organization of the day. But the originality of the cistercian reform resides especially in the fact that the traditional monastic observances were interpreted in an ascetic spirit. Total renunciation of the world, work, silence, and obedience to the abbot led to humility, that is, to becoming conscious of one's own misery. From there, the monk rose through mortification to the contemplation of divine Love, which alone could fill up that inner emptiness and restore in man the image of God distorted by sin. This ascent of the steps of love could be achieved only at the cost of ceaseless struggling and of a painful tension

[17]RB 48:7-8.

entailing daily suffering. Cistercian spirituality, especially with Aelred of Rievaulx, insisted a great deal on the redemptive value of suffering, which could lead the soul to heaven and accorded it, in this life, the certainty of eternal election. With Cîteaux, monasticism, though disputed and questioned from all sides, claimed to go on embodying the ideal of the primitive Church in all its purity. In actual fact, humility and penance, which were the spiritual masterwords of the apostolic movements, were reintegrated within benedictine monasticism by the white monks. But this convergence between the religious aspirations of the day and the cistercian message was to be short-lived. Though in Saint Bernard's time the cistercian order exerted an exceptional fascination on minds enamored of perfection and experienced very rapid growth, it soon lost sight of its primitive ideal, and signs of decay appeared as early as the second half of the twelfth century. The literalism the founders had claimed to banish soon reappeared, while the problems for which they had found no solution worsened: how could individual poverty be reconciled with collective wealth? How was it possible to be present to people while rejecting the world? To cite only one example: at a time when uncultivated rural spaces were becoming scarcer in the West, the Cistercians occasionally destroyed villages and drove away the peasants in order to create 'deserts' around their new foundations.[18]

This growing discrepancy between ideal and reality eventually tarnished the order's image. At the end of the twelfth century, a cistercian monk from Calabria, Joachim of Fiore, founded a reformed congregation called the order of Fiore. Its success remained limited, but Joachim's ideas were to exert great influence during the following decades. Starting from a meditation on the Book of Revelation and on the mystery of the Trinity, he foretold the imminent coming of

---

[18]As shown by R. A. Donkin, 'The Cistercian Order and the settlement of Northern England', *Geographic Review* 59 (1969) 403–416.

an age of the Holy Spirit, marked by the advent of a spiritual
Church, totally contemplative and pure, which was to spread
the 'eternal Gospel' throughout the earth. In so doing, this
mystical prophet showed his dissatisfaction with the ongoing
secularization of monasticism, and directed the most religious
minds towards the anticipation of a new world.

All in all, Cîteaux's spiritual heritage is not devoid of
ambiguity. At the level of its greatest representatives—Saint
Bernard, William of Saint Thierry, Aelred of Rievaulx and
many others—the cistercian school unquestionabley opened
up new avenues by emphasizing how rich were the ways of
union with God.[19] But by grounding this longing in a total
rejection of human nature and by making contempt for the
world into an absolute—whereas in the old monasticism it had
been tempered by a sense of moderation and by allowances for
individual needs—Cîteaux ran the danger of quickly becoming
estranged from the society around it and devoid of any hold
upon it. Its call for integral observance[20] of the rule often led
its monks to doctrinal and spiritual rigorism. By unilaterally
stressing asceticism and mortification, it doubtless contributed
to creating, among those who, within the order or outside
it, felt its influence, that somewhat strained religion, anxious at not having done enough, which is characteristic of
so many Christians, and indeed saints, in the twelfth and
thirteenth centuries.

THE LAITY IN SEARCH OF A SPIRITUALITY

The deep changes which occurred in the clerical world in
the late eleventh and early twelfth centuries could not leave

[19]See below, pp. 157ff.
[20]There is no really satisfactory translation for the term 'intégrisme,'
coined in France to describe right-wing movements which claim to strive
for an 'integral catholicism' and advocate both religious and socio-political
traditionalism. (Translator's note)

the laity indifferent. The gregorian reform did in fact cause an upheaval in church structures and challenged traditional hierarchies. During that restless period, monks such as Wederic in Flanders or William of Hirsau and his companions in southern Germany left their monasteries and launched on preaching campaigns against the antipope Guibert and his supporters. A few decades later, Saint Bernard himself would not hesitate to leave the cloister to combat the schism of Anacletus. Moreover, Gregory VII appealed several times to the laity, and especially to rulers and knights, to take measures against simoniacal clerics or concubinate priests, 'even by force if need be',[21] much to the displeasure of the clergy who, indignant at these unheard-of antics, blamed the pontiff for introducing subversion into the Church. Gregory rejected their accusations by emphasizing that all the faithful were called on to come to the aid of reform, provided they were in communion with Rome. Admittedly, his aim was not so much to favor the advancement of the laity as to extol the Apostolic See by directly committing the faithful to the authority of Peter's successor. But the appeal launched by Gregory VII and taken up again on another plane by Urban II at Clermont in 1095 no doubt contributed to increasing the role of the faithful within the Church; they were invited to put aside their passivity to offer their direct participation in reform and in the crusade. There had doubtless been lay religious movements during the preceding period, such as the Patarines of Milan and Florence. But they had remained relatively isolated and of little importance at the level of christendom. The new development which occurred at the end of the eleventh century was the masses' appearance on the scene—masses in which a longing for salvation was at work.

[21]Letter to Rodolphus of Schwaben, January 11, 1075, *Gregorii VII registrum*; ed. E. Caspar (1920) 104.

THE EMERGENCE OF CHRISTENDOM:
CRUSADES, EVANGELICAL MOVEMENTS, HERESIES

Under the influence of a pastoral ministry (*cura ani-marum*) which had improved thanks to the growing number of rural and urban parishes, and doubtless also to more frequent contacts with the world of religious at the level of priories and collegiate churches, the laity's religious spirit grew more refined in many parts of the West during the eleventh century. The spreading of the apostolic ideal by the canons, as well as the influence of hermits and of wandering preachers who propagated evangelical themes in their wake, contributed to awakening among the faithful a longing to rise to the spiritual level of the clerics and to achieve salvation without having to give up their state. The astounding success the call to the crusade launched by Urban II met with in all classes of society must no doubt be reset in this context. For the first time, indeed, the Church half-opened the floodgates of grace for the benefit of all the faithful, under the sole condition of going off to the East to battle against the enemies of Christ. Of course, the Clermont appeal was adressed primarily to the knights, whom it provided—as we have seen—both with a religious objective and with a justification of their state of life. But it was the rank and file that set out first and played a decisive role throughout the tribulations undergone by the frankish army from its arrival in Asia Minor to the fall of Jerusalem in 1099. The fact that thousands of men and women had taken to the road and had accepted harsh suffering for the love of God evidences that the masses had become deeply sensitive to the great spiritual themes of Christianity.

The objective set the crusaders by Urban II was twofold: assisting the Christians of the East and freeing Christ's tomb. The reward promised was plenary indulgence. For the crusade, armed pilgrimage that it was, did away with the punishment due for sin, and at the time held as important a place as confession in the penitential process: an offence was not deemed to have been totally remitted until it had been atoned for. Such perspectives were not indifferent to the crowds that set off at the call of popular preachers like Peter the Hermit, but alone they would doubtless not have been enough to awaken that great surge of devotion. That great horde of unarmed peasants, women, children, and clerics on the loose abandoned everything and left for the Holy Land less in order to gain the indulgence for the crusade than in the hope that the deliverance of the Holy Sepulchre would inaugurate a new era in the history of the Church and of the world. It is difficult to delineate the concrete notion they had of it, and the indications given by the chroniclers, all of whom were clerics inclined to report the masses' eschatological expectations in terms strongly marked by their own biblical culture, should not necessarily be taken literally. Did the crusaders really believe in the imminent coming of the antichrist and in the necessity of meeting him with that armed resistance of faith which would make Christ's final return possible? Did they really think that they would go directly from the earthly to the heavenly Jerusalem, from the Mount of Olives to paradise? There can be no doubt, in any case, that the popular membership of the crusade was animated by a messianic spirit and was convinced that the kingdom promised the lowly by the Gospel would arrive shortly. At the end of their pilgrimage was Jerusalem, the place where God's promises would be fulfilled, the blessed land where milk and honey would flow in abundance. Thus they found it normal to expect that in the Holy Land, along with the remission of their sins, they would obtain some remuneration for their labors as first fruits of their reward in the world to come.

Moreover, the masses who answered the call of the crusade preachers were convinced that God had assigned them a task—the liberation of the holy places—and, more broadly, the mission of purifying the world from evil so as to prepare his glorious return. Hence the massacres of Jews, and to a lesser degree of Saracens, which especially marked the first two crusades—those in which popular participation was the strongest. On a par with heresy, the refusal of baptism was viewed by the ordinary faithful as an insult to God which was liable to bring down his wrath upon men. In their eyes, the Kingdom must be accessible only to the pure and humble whom God had chosen as his spokesmen. Before the fall of Jerusalem, the chroniclers depict the 'little people of the host' as setting right the barons, who were inclined to consider only their political interests and to give their ambitions first place. In the eyes of these poor folk, the true weapons which would bring victory to the Christians were penance (whose sign was the cross worn on their clothes), fasts, prayers and processions. By exterminating God's enemies, but also by inflicting suffering and mortification on themselves, all contributed their own bit to hastening the liberation of Christ's tomb and the coming of his kingdom. This state of mind may be likened to that of the followers of the genuinely apostolic life (*vita vere apostolica*) during the same period. Had not Saint Norbert, founder of Prémontré, stated: 'poverty puts us even now in possession of the kingdom of heaven'? Refracted through various mentalities and backgrounds, the same spiritual themes permeated all the consciences of the time.

The crusades revealed the existence of a popular spirituality for the first time in the West; it emerged all at once as a coherent whole. Its component elements include, first of all, devotion to Christ, which gave rise to a longing to free the land where he had once lived and to avenge God's honor, which the infidels had flaunted. Add to this a yearning for individual and collective purification, which accounts both for the crusade's penitential aspects and for its messianic dimensions; but the eschatology impelling that great movement was directed less towards anticipation than towards action. The people of God, and especially the poorest of them—who were also the holiest—, regarded themselves as invested with a mission which had a meaning in the history of salvation: 'God's deeds through the Franks' (*Gesta Dei per Francos*), as Guibert of Nogent did not hesitate to write. By his struggle against the enemies of the faith, by the harshness of the penances he inflicted on himself, the crusader won heaven, so to speak, by the sweat of his brow. Grace poured itself out beyond sacramental mediations, and the Church was looked upon as a supervisory and organizational structure rather than a dispenser of the divine favors. As a high point of spiritual life, the crusade met with immense success because it answered the expectations of the faithful who yearned for a salvation which seemed hard to achieve in daily life. The 1096-1099 upsurge was the first of a series of great devotional movements which were to follow one after another until the end of the Middle Ages. From the crusades to the fourteenth-century processions of flagellants, the religious life of the laity was indeed to be marked by an alternation between spurts of spiritual enthusiasm which periodically shook christendom, and a conformist, routine-minded practice whose level was, generally speaking, mediocre. By highlighting the great moments of collective exaltation, we run the risk of lapsing into a romantic view of the faith of these Christians. By considering only the practices and observances of ordinary times, we lay ourselves open to seeing no more than its shortcomings and of neglecting one of its essential dimensions.

Important as their place was in the religious life of twelfth-century men and women, the crusades nonetheless remained exceptional events. There were four great crusades between 1096 and 1204, and the very enthusiasm they unleashed was in proportion to their rarity. Moreover, for reasons which were not all base, many of the faithful could not consider leaving their homeland for long periods, sometimes with no hope of returning. In the case of many who stayed behind or who came back, a deepened faith expressed itself in increased demands on the clergy, which often took the form of virulent anticlericalism. When all was said and done, the gregorian reform had remained a matter for clerics. Once the worst of the crisis was over, the layfolk whose assistance Gregory VII had required were sent back to their worldly business (*secularia negotia*) and invited to fall back into line. Fervent religious forces suddenly found themselves unemployed. They did not easily allow themselves to be brought to heel. The very success of the reform had brought about an expansion of church property, thus anchoring in the faithful the conviction that throughout the whole affair, the clergy had pursued no more than its own advantage. From then on, the laity's criticism shifted from morals to money: in the twelfth century, clerics were blamed less for their failings in chastity than for their wealth and power. Under the influence of such popular preachers as Peter the Hermit or Robert of Arbrissel and his disciples, who spread abroad the great watchwords of the Gospel and especially the message of the Beatitudes, the peasants and burghers of northern and western France attacked both their pastors and the black monks: they wanted the clergy to be poor and apostolic, that is, capable of announcing the word of God to the faithful; they demanded that its lifestyle and behavior be in keeping with the precepts of the Gospel. Such protests were ambiguous, the more so since, in the cities, the simoniacal bishops whom the faithful took on were often also their lords. But religious motivations should not be ruled out for all that: in the face of the mediocre compromises in which the cause of reform became bogged down after Paschal II, a popular evangelism asserted itself. It inspired many religious movements, both orthodox and heretical.

Their common denominator was voluntary poverty. This basic option seemed the necessary condition of faithfulness to Christ 'who had nowhere to lay his head'. But it also took on an exemplary significance, given the economic and social realities of the time. In a world where the rapid development of production and trade was deepening the cleavages within rural society and giving rise to new forms of destitution, the choice of poverty as a way of life indicated a wish to draw nearer to the castaways of expansion and to those who were shut out by society: wanderers, prostitutes, lepers, and others. It was also a protest against the luxury of the mighty, most especially of the church hierarchy. It was at this time that exposure of the roman curia's corruption became a commonplace of religious writings, as may be seen in Saint Bernard's *Five Books On Consideration* (*De consideratione*) or in the fiery sermons of

Arnold of Brescia. Such protest was understandable in an age when the process of centralization which had been underway since the late eleventh century was beginning to dislocate the episcopal framework to the benefit of the papal court. But the institutional aspect of that phenomenon was not the one most clearly perceived at the time. Both among great spiritual teachers and among ordinary faithful, the idea prevailed that the Church could not be true to its mission unless it went back to evangelical poverty, through the practice of which it would be able to avoid lapsing into a contradiction between ideal and lived reality.

In fact, such aspirations were quickly disappointed, for the times were not ripe for a poor and servant Church. Exactly during the twelfth century, the gregorian reform had left the church materially wealthier and endowed with an influence upon society which reached a hitherto unequaled level. Far from developing in the direction the evangelical movements had hoped for, its power apparatus was only reinforced. More-over, after a short-lived attempt under Paschal II, renunciation of its possessions by the clergy was more than ever out of the question. Several factors operated in this direction, the main one being the spontaneous tendency of the minds of the time to equate pre-eminence in dignity with splendor and wealth. In a Church in which clerics sat as kings, it was fitting that their lifestyle display the eminent dignity of their state. Even among the advocates of reform, many were far from considering the clerical ownership of property as an evil. The case of the regular canon Gerhoh of Reichersberg (1093-1169) is typical in this regard: an open, progressive mind, opposed to the 'feudalization' of the clergy, he nevertheless asserted, especially in writings after 1130, that the Church would be irremediably weakened were it to give up its lands and rights. It would, indeed, no longer be able to fulfill its duty to aid the poor, and particularly those religious whose living conditions were precarious. Thus he simply wished ecclesiastical revenues to be more fairly distributed and to go first of all to the poverty-stricken. Only a materially prosperous Church would be able to develop works of charity and guarantee to those who had chosen voluntary poverty the free exercise of their vocation.

Moreover, by a strange backlash, those very persons within the Church who had professed destitution were soon the victims—or the beneficiaries, according to one's point of view—of what Georges Duby has called 'the paradoxes of the monastic economy'. The Cistercians, for instance, as well as some congregations of canons regular belonging to the new observance (*ordo novus*), had unknowingly chosen a model of economic activity only too well fitted to the new conditions of production and trade. At a time when land rents brought in little and when the reduction of statute labor was forcing lords to resort to paid workers, the agricultural concerns of the new orders, which refused to employ tenants and had free labor available to them in the persons of laybrothers, found themselves in a privileged situation. Moreover, their ascetic vocation favored the expansion of highly productive rural tracts, located in solitary, untilled places marked out for a farming system based on forestry and pasturage. Having become great producers of wool and meat, the white monks and their imitators did not hesitate to exchange the surpluses they produced for money, and progressed very rapidly on the way to wealth.

This prosperity very soon constrasted, in a manner scandalous to the eyes of the world, with the deep austerity of their lives. In the long run, the economic results of monastic reform laid the groundwork for the condemnation of monasticism in both its renewed and its traditional form.[22]

At the very moment when bishops and religious were falling into the trap of expansion, the Church was issuing multiple warnings against the new forms of economic activity, particularly against trading in money. The rapid development

[22]Georges Duby, 'Le monachisme et l'économie rurale', in *Hommes et structures du Moyen Age* (Paris, 1973) 392.

of production and trade stimulated among lay people, as among many clerics, a thirst for gain and profit which was apt to degenerate into a spirit of lucre. Hence the repeated and constantly reinforced condemnations of loaning money at interest, which was equated with usury, and even of chattel mortgaging: the latter was prohibited by the Council of Tours presided over by Pope Alexander III in 1163. Moreover, Gratian's *Decretals*, drawn up around 1140 and soon to compel recognition as the Church's legal code, declared that 'only with difficulty and in very few cases can a merchant be pleasing to God.' Though it is not our aim to study the evolution of canon law in the face of financial and economic realities, we must nevertheless stress its repercussions on the spiritual plane. In the hierarchy of vices, for instance, avarice (*avaritia*), that is, both unbridled seeking after profit and selfish hoarding, more and more frequently stole the lead from pride (*superbia*) as the twelfth century advanced. At this time, as Lester K. Little has aptly shown, the theme of the usurer plunged into hell, treasure in hand, became very common in iconography.[23] It played the same role as had the pugnacious and undisciplined knight in the previous century and constituted the new embodiment of the forces of evil which stood ready to crush the poor and the weak. This conviction is also expressed in such spiritual treatises as the *Fourth Vigil of the Night* (*De quarta vigilia noctis*) by the regular canon Gerhoh of Reichersberg, written around 1165. He has the third age of the world begin with Gregory VII and places it under the sign of avarice, which, in his eyes, was the major problem of his time. In actual fact, won over by wealth while at the same time hostile to the new activities which made currency into something more than a mere instrument of measurement and exchange, the twelfth-century Church

[23]Lester K. Little, 'Pride goes before Avarice: Social Change and the Vices in Latin Christendom', *The American Historical Review* 76 (1971) 16–49.

did not succeed in defining a consistent line of conduct with
regard to money. This was not without consequences for
the spiritual life of the laity. Scandalized by the wealth of
certain clerics while at the same time paralyzed in their own
activities by canonical prohibitions and by the disapprobation
weighing on advanced forms of trade, many of them suffered
pangs of conscience or, worse still, were racked by the fear
of damnation. Such uneasiness was experienced especially in
the cities and particularly in Italy, where the precocious development of a monetary economy caused tensions to appear
earlier than elsewhere.

A second question also gave rise to difficulties between
clergy and laity: access to the divine Word, with which
the faithful increasingly wished to acquaint themselves directly. But its transmission remained a monopoly of the clerics, whose knowledge of it was generally inadequate. Those
who had been through the schools—and they were few in
number—judged that making Scripture accessible to lay people was a serious danger, for the latter, uncultivated as they
were, ran the risk of interpreting it incorrectly: 'Like a pearl
before swine', wrote curial official Walter Map around 1185,
'shall the Word be given to simple souls whom we know are
incapable of receiving it, and still more incapable of giving
what they have received? This may not be, and it must be
ruled out.'[24] This is a very revealing reaction: many clerics
viewed the Bible as a treasure which they were in charge of
keeping and of passing on intact, rather than as a message
to be disclosed and proclaimed. Thus they were suspicious of
the vernacular translations of the Gospel which appeared in
many places during the second half of the twelfth century.
The Church was doubtless concerned with maintaining orthodoxy in doctrine, but the desire to preserve its role as the
necessary mediator between God and the faithful must have
had something to do with its attitude.

[24]Walter Map, *De nugis curialium* 1.31.

In actual fact, as early as the end of the eleventh century, hermits who had not received even minor orders were seen to lay claim to the ministry of the Word without their bishop's permission. Bernard of Tiron, for instance, who in western France gathered crowds of peasants come to hear his sermons, answered a priest who disputed his right to preach by claiming that this was obtained by the virtue of mortification. Such an answer is significant: it implies that leading a way of life in keeping with the Gospel guarantees the authenticity of the Word and allows one to announce it to the people. Most of the great popular preachers of the early twelfth century, from Robert of Arbrissel to Saint Norbert, eventually received permission to preach (*licentia praedicandi*) from the pope, and this shielded them from all attacks. The fact remains, however, that in the eyes of the faithful it was their personal sanctity, rather than the regularity of their canonical situation, which entitled these men to speak to them about God with authority. Thus many lay persons soon claimed the right of announcing the Word. They were dubbed 'pseudo-prophets' by the clergy and the hierarchy, both of whom were very sensitive to the risk of heresy. In 1140, Gratian's *Decretals* sanctioned this hostile attitude by prescribing 'that in the presence of clerics lay people should not presume to give any teaching, unless at the request of the former'.

Given that lay people generally experienced difficulty in discovering a spirituality suited to their state, the question was particularly acute in the case of women, who came up against additional obstacles. Spiritual literature, like theology, was the work of clerics, inclined by their entire formation towards misogyny. Under the influence of Saint Jerome and of a patristic tradition hostile to women, the clergy presented women primarily as daughters of Eve, the root of all evil and the main agent of sin. In the eyes of ecclesiastical writers, women became worthy of interest and respect only when they possessed manly qualities. Hence the praise they awarded queens or empresses who, by their firm conduct, had succeeded in living down the weakness peculiar to their sex.

Forms of religious life for women did indeed exist: besides a few recluses shut up in their cells, many nuns led pious lives in community under the Rule of Saint Benedict. But admission into a monastery was in most cases conditioned by the payment of a dowry, and this in fact instituted a *numerus clausus*. Moreover, though consecrated virgins and widows enjoyed some regard, this was not the case with married women. Those who belonged to the upper aristocracy might be able to play some part in the religious life of their time by favoring the Church and multiplying monastic foundations, but this privilege was restricted to a small number of great ladies. All in all, married women had scarcely any religious prospects, and marriage tended to appear rather as a handicap as far as salvation was concerned. In the clerics' eyes sexual life was a consequence of sin, and marital relations, which could be tolerated for reproductive purposes alone, always constituted an offence—at least a venial one—to the extent that they were accompanied by pleasure. Not to be a source of sin, carnal acts had to be accomplished only reluctantly, and Saint Peter Damian merely illustrated this widespread mentality by speaking highly to lay people of the elephant which, 'impelled to the act of propagation, turns its head away, showing thereby that it is acting under compulsion from nature, against its will, and that it is ashamed and disgusted at what it is doing'.[25] Married people were therefore to approach Holy Communion rarely, and in any case they had to abstain from all carnal relations before receiving the sacrament. If they truly wished to achieve salvation, they had to live in continence: 'To observe chastity once children have been born is a great thing', wrote a flemish hagiographer around 1130. It was even better to separate in order that each partner might enter a monastery. Such a practice was common at the time: many women were forced to become nuns against their will to

---

[25] *Ep.* 1.15, quoted by R. Bultot in *I laici nella 'Societas christiana' dei secoli XI e XII* (Milan, 1968) 391.

allow their husbands to satisfy their longings for perfection. In an admittedly somewhat special context, this was the case with Heloise, who became abbess of the Paraclete after Abelard had entered monastic life, and who, from the recesses of her abbey, sent him letters aflame with passion.

The general climate of uneasiness which prevailed among lay people accounts for the success met with by evangelical movements. In the late eleventh and early twelfth centuries, the movements were still very much marked by the keywords of the gregorian reform. Their initiators were usually clerics such as Robert of Arbrissel, Vitalis of Savigny or the monk Henry of Lausanne, who drew crowds by their personalities and the content of their preaching. Indeed, they presented the Gospel as the sole rule of life for Christians and insisted on the fact that the clergy were eminently bound to conform to it. From moral rigorism, many went on to negate the traditional categories of faithful (*ordines*) within the Church: when it came to the demands of the Gospel, were not all the baptized on an equal footing? The lay people who joined these movements no longer tolerated being excluded from the call to sanctity on account of living in the world. Refusing to be merely objects of the clerics' pastoral ministry, they too sought to lead a religious life and longed for a faith that would carry Christ's message to the level of action. Among them were many women. The clerics who spoke of them usually described them as fanatics, mad about their bodies and having hopeless morals. The reality is not so simple: we have only to consider the enthusiasm aroused by hermits like Stephen of Obazine or preachers like Tanchelm or Saint Norbert among both prostitutes and great ladies of the aristocracy who followed them to the 'desert', much to the outrage of right-thinking people. Little eventually remained of all this excitement: a few double monasteries in the orders founded respectively in England in 1131 by Saint Gilbert of Sempringham, and at Fontevrault by Robert of Arbrissel. The latter placed both communities—the men's and the women's—under the authority of an abbess, who was to be

a widow, not a virgin. But the order of Fontevrault was not
slow in developing along the same lines as traditional women's
monasteries, and as early as a few decades after its foundation
only members of the upper nobility were able to enter it. In
the twelfth century, female religious orders did not yet exist;
women's monasteries were in a state of spiritual and material
subjection to the male orders to which they belonged. This
illustrates the difficulty women experienced in fulfilling their
spiritual destiny without following in the wake of men.

In the course of the twelfth century, the evangelical movements went ever further and soon entered open conflict with
the Church. With Arnold of Brescia, who won great popular
success in Rome by condemning the wealth of priests and the
splendor of the Curia, the theme of poverty took first place.
In his view, since the clergy had rendered itself unworthy
by refusing to give up its possessions, hierarchy had to be
rejected and all the baptized regarded as equal. Only actual
fidelity to the Gospel entitled one to exercise authority within
the Church. Casting discredit on priests and pastors was soon
followed by criticism of the sacraments, with the demand
that they be simplified. For both the supporters of Henry
of Lausanne and the Arnoldists or 'Poor of Lombardy', the
universal priesthood of the faithful made ordination superfluous and a common confession of offences took the place of
penance. Having gone on from anticlerical polemics to calling
the Church into question, the adepts of the evangelical life
were reaching the brink of heresy.

As early as the eleventh century, as we have noted, centers of heresy had appeared in the West. But they were
few in number and quickly contained, and did not develop
much. In the twelfth century, the phenomenon attained much
greater numerical importance, to the point of challenging the
Church's influence in some areas. Our aim here is not to
retrace the history of these religious currents, or even to study
their doctrines. We need only bring out the reasons for their
success, and particularly the spiritual motivations which led
many lay persons to join them.

Such motivations are not always easy to grasp. We hardly know these movements except through what their opponents said about them, and it is sometimes difficult to arrive at a precise notion of the content of their beliefs. However, reports gleaned from various sides—from Soissons to Cologne and from Toulouse to Milan—make it possible to distinguish in the twelfth-century heresies two main currents.[26] One of them insisted primarily on the necessary coincidence between the word of the Gospel and activity to fulfill it in the world. Its followers set out to combat the decadence of the Church by forming groups of fervent Christians on its fringes. Their refusal of existing structures did not call the dogmatic foundations of Christianity into question except on points of detail. This was the tendency that prevailed in most of the popular movements of the first half of the century, and later among the Waldenses, or Poor of Lyon, a group of lay people condemned in 1184 for having preached without a mandate from their bishop—for in their opinion the practice of apostolic life and especially of poverty conferred the right to proclaim the Gospel. The conflict was a disciplinary rather than a doctrinal one, at least in the beginning, and some Waldenses did in fact return to the Catholic Church in the early twelfth century.

The second current, which intensified after 1140, no doubt under the influence of oriental contributions, particularly from the Bogomils of Bosnia and Bulgaria, was set off from the first by its clearly dualistic character. These latter heretics were described by their opponents as Manicheans; to us they are known by the name Cathars. They stated that the necessary renewal of Christianity must be accompanied by a questioning of the entire body of doctrine taught by the Church. In their view, indeed, the Church had concealed, for its own advantage, the revolutionary truth hidden in the New Testament, that is, the permanent opposition and struggle

[26]As was aptly demonstrated by Raoul Manselli in his basic work, *L'eresia del male* (Naples, 1963) 118–149.

between God and Satan, Good and Evil. The good principle was the mainspring of the world of the spirit, whereas the evil principle—rebel son or fallen angel—had created the material world and the flesh. In this viewpoint, human souls were fragments of spirit entangled in matter, from which they had to extricate themselves at all costs. They were assisted in this effort by the example of Christ, greatest of angels or best of humans, whom God had adopted as his son. He had come into this world, but neither his flesh nor his Passion had been anything but appearances. Jesus had redeemed humankind not through his suffering, but through his teaching. The Old Testament was the work of the powers of Evil and was therefore worthless; the Gospel alone was divine.

There is not time here to try to give an account of cathar dogma with all its subtleties and variations, from mitigated dualism to absolute dualism, nor to reflect on the deep meaning of its cosmogony. But we must seek to explain the fascination exerted by these beliefs on a very large number of men and women, especially in the south of France and in Italy, between the mid-twelfth and mid-thirteenth centuries. The apparent simplicity of the doctrine and the sobriety of its liturgy must have worked in its favor. More important, it seems, was the distinction between the Perfect, bound to strict asceticism, and the ordinary faithful, who in practice enjoyed great freedom of morals and could engage in any activity at all, provided that before their death they received the *consolamentum*, a laying on of hands which wrested them from the material world and awakened them to the life of the spirit. Many women were also led to adhere to the heresy because it afforded them the possibility of equal treatment with men. There was indeed quite a large number of Perfect women, and some of them even lived in convents of sorts, such as the one at Prouille in Languedoc.

Beyond their differences, the evangelical and dualistic currents have in common their refusal to consider salvation as dependent on the mediation of the visible Church and the institutional priesthood. More deeply, they professed the same exacerbated spiritualism, which could just as well lead to the rejection of tithes as to the negation of some sacraments. It is rather disconcerting to a modern mind that evangelism should result in a pessimistic attitude towards all forms of life, and in particular towards procreation. Paradoxically, hatred of the visible Church and the desire to dissociate oneself from the established order of things led to a more pronounced rejection of the world and of the flesh than had ever existed within monasticism. But perhaps the key to the attraction exercised by the heresies, and especially by catharism, lies in the spiritual evolution previously analyzed. At a time when the Church, at least its clergy, had clearly chosen to act upon the world and to place it under its guardianship in order to bring it into conformity with God's plan, many faithful chose to protest against this evolution by asserting their faithfulness to a paleo-Christianity based on evangelical simplicity and rejection of the world. If we accept this hypothesis, catharism would be the ultimate metamorphosis of monastic spirituality, popularized and distorted by its faithful, at a time when many clerics were turning away from it and when the Church was adjusting all too well to a political and cultural conjuncture which operated in its favor. Far from being the religion of new times, as some would have it, it seems instead to express a refusal to change. For by denying the reality of Christ's human nature and of the Passion—which they regarded as mere appeareances, the Cathars did away with the Incarnation. In spite of their professed attachment to the New Testament, they were going against the tide of the movement which, since the eleventh century, had impelled Christians to live the Gospel in time and within the world. Christianity's real response to the challenge of the dualistic heresies was not the Inquisition, but the development of a spirituality which, while not underestimating the corrupting effects of sin, asserted the goodness and the beauty of creation and stressed the necessary bond between suffering and Redemption.

This result was not achieved in a day, for in this area
medieval clerics found it very difficult to free themselves from
generally accepted notions. Under the twofold influence of
monastic tradition and ancient philosophy, they long held
to the superiority of contemplation over action and of consecrated life over life in the world. In the twelfth century,
the evolution of society and of mentalities began to render
such clear-cut contrasts obsolete. Many among the faithful
longed to live their christian vocation in the world, without
having to deny the basic values of their state. This often
stormy confrontation between a theoretical teaching less and
less in touch with reality and the concrete experiences of the
laity gave rise to the fundamental tensions which marked the
spiritual life of the West during the twelfth century.

One of the main problems facing the men and women of
the period was that of work. In the climate of toil and effort—
from the clearing of land to the expansion of industry—
characteristic of western society at the time, it took on considerable importance. It was a means of development, but also,
and increasingly, a source of profit. The Church, for its part,
hesitated between a pessimistic vision supported by texts from
Genesis, where work was presented as the direct consequence
of sin, and a more positive notion based on some passages
from Saint Paul[27] and on the Greek Fathers, particularly Saint
John Chrysostom.

During the early Middle Ages, the first of these two notions
had generally prevailed, and manual labor had been regarded
as a penance. The Rule of Saint Benedict had afforded it a
rather broad place: inasmuch as it required tiresome effort,
it was a privileged means of atonement and sanctification for
the monk. Monastic spirituality viewed work especially as a
remedy against idleness, one of the most dangerous snares
laid by the fiend for those aspiring to perfection. 'Undertake

---

[27]The most important text in this regard is 2 Th 2:10: 'let [no] one
have any food if he refuse[s] to do any work.'

some task so that the devil will always find you busy', had
been Saint Jerome's advice to the monk Rusticus, 'for it does
not befit the mind to wander off into evil thoughts.' This
rather negative notion of work found itself reinforced during
the feudal era. Aristocratic society, indeed, considered manual
activity an occupation only just good enough for serfs, and
the old roman ideal of dignified leisure (*otium cum digni-
tate*) continued—though in a very different social context—
to exert a deep fascination on the elite, as witnessed by the
development of court life in the twelfth century. At Cluny,
around 1100, the monks hardly worked with their hands any
longer, except inasmuch as they engaged in specialized tasks
such as copying and illuminating manuscripts. The constantly
reasserted superiority of contemplative life over active life even
allowed Peter the Venerable to maintain that by replacing
manual work with other obligations he was remaining faithful
to the spirit of the benedictine rule. The religious movements
based on the ideal of the apostolic life do not register any
noteworthy change in this regard. The clerics who practised
voluntary poverty considered themselves under no obligation
to work for a living but should dedicate themselves entirely to
their pastoral tasks. Some of them even resorted to begging, in
which they saw both a means of remuneration for the apostle
and an example of humility for the faithful. 'In order that
they may eat, they preach', as a priest of the time wrote
on the subject of hermits and other wandering preachers
(*Wanderprediger*): he disliked them and was scandalized by
such unfair competition.

Finally, the Church looked askance at the development of
professions considered illicit or dangerous (such as merchants,
or money-changers) and of societies of workers—the first
'guilds'—which were then forming on the basis of professional
specialization and outside the framework of acknowledged social hierarchies. In such a climate of suspicion, urban workers
in search of recognition for their place in society, but also
their spiritual dignity, came up against a resistance which was
to yield only slowly.

In the long run, however, social change and the renewal
of theology, which made contact once more with its greek
sources, caused the clerics' mindset to progress. The ideology
of the three roles—priests, warriors and workers—operated
positively in this regard by assigning to each category (*ordo*)
a place in christian society. We have already shown earlier how
the lay aristocracy, by means of the knightly ideal and holy
warfare, had been offered the possibility of achieving salvation
by exercising the duties of its state. The workers were to encounter more difficulty in bringing clerics to acknowledge the
religious value of their activities. They did, however, succeed
to some extent by way of their social role.

Honorius of Autun, an author devoid of originality but
whose witness is all the more valuable because it reflects
general opinion, writes on the subject of peasants: 'A great
number of them will be saved because they live simply and
feed the people of God by the sweat of their brow.' In the
course of the twelfth century, the sociological pattern of
three-part society compelled recognition throughout christendom and relegated the canonical distinctions and spiritual
hierarchies implied by the division of the baptized into monks,
clerics and lay people to second place. That pattern itself
evolved toward more complex forms as economic and social
structures became more diversified. Thus the list of 'estates
of the world' constantly grew longer, while participation in
the common good provided sufficient justification for many
forms of human activity. Such a change in perspective eventually called traditional notions of the degrees of perfection
into question. As early as the mid-twelfth century, Anselm
of Havelberg emphasized that the way of life chosen—in the
world or outside it—was less important than the manner in
which every human being behaved in his or her state, for God
made no distinction between classes of people. But placing the
ordinary faithful on an equal footing with the clerics did not
yet mean acknowledging the existence of a spirituality proper
to their state. And that was precisely where the difficulty lay.

The example of work is very significant in this regard. It was, as a matter of fact, brought back into honor by the new monasticism, and especially by the Cistercians. 'Rise up from rest to work'[28], wrote Saint Bernard to a cluniac monk whom he wished to draw to Clairvaux. The question was indeed at the heart of the controversy between black and white monks: the latter asserted that there could be no true monastic life unless the religious engaged in real and useful manual labor. Moreover, the laybrother institution, ambiguous though it was, implied a new attitude toward work, viewed as a possible means of sanctification. Finally, we have already pointed out the importance of the theoretical debate between regular canons and monks over the relationship between the active and contemplative lives: Christ praised Mary out of pure charity, wrote Anselm of Havelberg in this connection, in order to avoid Martha's waxing too triumphant—for basically she was right. Besides, according to him, one should imitate, neither Martha nor Mary, but Christ himself, who was primarily active in that the better part of his life was devoted to teaching and preaching. But this new appraisal of work in the world of religious did not provide a satisfying answer to the problems of the laity. Even among the Cistercians, the monks' work remained primarily a penitential, and to some extent a symbolic, activity. It was far from sufficient to ensure the community's livelihood; that was provided mainly by the laybrothers. For the ordinary faithful, who had to provide for their needs themselves, the terms of the question were different. It was a matter of gaining recognition for the spiritual dignity of work and for its positive value as a means of salvation. As Jacques Le Goff has aptly shown, this was the direction in which 'the pressure of the new professional classes—merchants, artisans, workmen—concerned with finding a justification for their activity, for their calling, on the

[28] *Surge de otio ad laborem.*

religious plane... not in spite of their profession but through their profession'[29] exercised itself.

This diffuse aspiration was more strongly experienced in the cities, where the rapid development of industry and trade had created a lay environment which was both dynamic and full of fighting spirit. It should come as no surprise that forms of religious life of a new kind, suited to the spiritual concerns of the laity, appeared first of all in the great merchant cities of Italy. The most interesting case is that of the Humiliati, originally a group of artisans leading a life of work and prayer in community, which appeared in Milan around 1175 and spread throughout Lombardy. These pious layfolk were workers who, while continuing to exercise their professional activities—in general they were weavers—and to lead a family life in their houses, led an austere existence and abstained from swearing as well as from initiating lawsuits. Excommunicated in 1184 for having preached in public without permission, they were reinstated in the Church in 1199 by Innocent III, who divided them into three orders: the first two were genuine religious subject to a rule, the remaining one a kind of third order before the term was coined. Its members lived in the world according to a *propositum*, that is, a set of statutes defining their form of life. Beyond these canonical distinctions, that which united the various groups of Humiliati and made for their originality was the importance the practise of a trade held in their daily existence: its purpose was to enable them to provide for their needs and to exercise charity towards the poor. Although, later on, they eventually became wealthy themselves and lost sight of their primitive ideal, the Humiliati were nonetheless the first lay group to have combined work, viewed as a real means of earning a living, with an intense life of prayer. Similar

[29]Jacques Le Goff, 'Métier et profession d'après les manuels de confesseurs au Moyen Age', in *Beitrage zum Berufsbewusstsein des Mittelalterlichen Menschen* (Berlin, 1964) 53.

tendencies may be observed in the communities of beguines which began to multiply in Brabant and Flanders at the end of the twelfth century. The Church granted these aspirations a kind of official consecration in 1199 by canonizing a draper, Saint Homobonus of Cremona, a genuine representative of the little folk (*popolo*) of the italian communes.

A similar development occurred as regards marriage. For centuries the married state had been judged incompatible with a religious life. Here again traditional notions were called into question, one small stroke at a time. Honorius of Autun, whose importance we have already noted as a faithful echo of the concerns of his time, referred to husbands and wives who led saintly lives in marriage as 'good spouses' (*boni conjugati*). More significant still, Pope Alexander III in 1175, acknowledged for the first time, that the ancient canons relating to the continence of the married faithful on fast days could be considered mere counsels rather than precepts. He went even further in a bull addressed to the master of the Knights of Saint James, a society of knights and clerics formed in Spain for the purpose of defending Christians against the Moors. Since most of its lay members were married, the question of their canonical status had been raised. The pontiff put an end to the controversy which had arisen on the subject by asserting that the state of perfection was not bound to virginity. Married or not, the knights of Saint James could rightly be considered religious inasmuch as they had made vows of obedience and exposed themselves to the dangers of battle in a spirit of sacrifice.[30] The importance of such a decision was considerable: by displacing the center of gravity of religious life from celibacy to obedience and penance, it removed the main obstacle preventing married faithful from having access to it. Thus the following decades witnessed the appearance of numerous groups of men and women who led

---

[30]Cf. E.G. Blanco, *The Rule of the Spanish Military Order of St. James, 1170–1493* (Leiden, 1971) 171.30.

a pious life in common. The Humiliati of Lombardy, the rural penitents who appeared in northern Italy around 1180, the beguines and beghards of the Low Countries advocated equality between the sexes in the Church and claimed the right to live an authentic christian existence within their families. The ideal of flight from the world was interiorized: it ceased to be a rejection of matter and the flesh and became a struggle against all forms of sin, from which no category of Christians was disqualified by its state of life.

More generally speaking, the laity no longer defined itself solely as the sum total of those faithful who lacked the powers of order and jurisdiction, but as a working component of the internal dynamism of the Church. This new attitude on the part of lay people brought them into conflict with the hierarchy several times, particularly over proclaiming the Gospel. Exercising the ministry of the Word without a licence from the bishop was in fact considered a sacrilegious encroachment by the clergy. Had such activites not been enough to entail the condemnation of Valdes and, in his wake, of the Poor of Lyon and of Lombardy? Here again, pressure on the part of the religious elite eventually, on the threshold of the thirteenth century, forced the recognition of new rights. Innocent III, so to speak, defused a situation that had become explosive by distinguishing between two kinds of texts in Scripture: on one hand, the plain ones (*aperta*), that is, the narrative episodes and morality tales which abounded in Bible stories and were readily accessible to all; on the other hand, the profound passages (*profunda*), or dogmatic expositions, whose complexities clerics alone were able to understand (for instance, most of the Gospel of Saint John and of the Book of Revelation). These two levels of revelation were matched by two quite distinct forms of public speaking: moral and penitential exhortation and preaching properly so called, which clarified the mysteries of the faith. Lay people had spontaneously embarked on the first path: the Waldenses, the Humiliati[31] and soon the Penitents of Assisi around Saint Francis, called the faithful to conversion and prayer in a direct, down-to-earth style not unlike that which was customary in town assemblies. They did not shirk from taking on those whose behavior stood in the way of the Gospel: usurers, unworthy clerics, bishops more concerned with ensuring their party's victory than with securing peace, and so forth. This possibility of declaring the essentials of the christian message and of seeing to its implementation in political and social life was an important conquest of the evangelical movements. It would be left to the mendicant orders, in the thirteenth century, to draw all the consequences and to reestablish the bond between moral admonition and theological discourse.

At the end of the twelfth century, the main obstacles to the fulfillment of a christian vocation in the world had been overcome or were on the way to being overcome. Does it follow, then, that the specific elements of the lay state— particularly work and married life—had become positive values through which the faithful could attain perfection? The answer to this question is not simple, for the Church's attitude toward earthly realities had not shed all its ambiguities. The case of Saint Homobonus deserves closer scrutiny, for it is exemplary in this regard. The fact that the pope canonized a merchant is certainly of great importance, since the entire spiritual and canonical tradition of the previous centuries had been marked by great mistrust of the profession, to say the least. But a reading of the bull of canonization shows that Homobonus was considered a saint primarily because he had given up running a profitable business and had distributed his possessions to the poor, while firmly resisting the heretics

---

[31]To quote Cardinal James of Vitry (1165–1240): 'The Humiliati who have given up everything for Christ come together in various places, living by the work of their hands, frequently preaching the word of God and listening to it willingly. Their faith is as deep as it is solid and their action is effective.' (James of Vitry, *Letters*, ed. Huyghens, p.72.)

of his native town. It is as though he had sanctified himself not through the exercise of his professional activity but rather in spite of it, or in any case after having abandoned it. And when, in the thirteenth century, the clergy and people of some lombard cities spontaneously 'canonized' genuine 'worker saints', their initiatives received no approval whatsoever on the part of Rome. The same could be said of married life, which, to the Christians of the time, seemed even less likely than work to offer much in the way of spiritual prospects. Though some saints of the period were married men and fathers, their family life had little to do with the reputation surrounding them. We can hardly blame their contemporaries for remaining indifferent to that aspect of things: there was no spirituality of marriage until Saint Francis de Sales, whereas the spirituality of work is a twentieth-century invention. It is, however, appropriate to point out these limitations, which from an historian's viewpoint are perfectly explicable: within the context of an economy which, in most cases, barely ensured human subsistence, men and women of the time would have needed rare gifts of abstraction and imagination to see in their labor a continuation of the work of creation.

For most lay people, therefore, the way of access to sanctity was neither work nor family life but rather the practise of charity, which, in the twelfth century, took on new forms and new meaning. Almsgiving has always held an important place in christian life, of course, and carolingian clerics had already insisted a great deal on this point in the exhortations they addressed to layfolk. But following the West's economic revival, we witness a genuine revolution of charity and the emergence of an authentic spirituality concerning it. This was based on devotion to Christ, and especially to his humanity. It was for the love of him 'who had nowhere to lay his head' that the destitute were aided; they were henceforth termed 'Christ's poor' (*pauperes Christi*), an expression which during the previous century had referred instead to religious. This mystical partiality for poverty was a new occurrence in the history of western spirituality. Until the twelfth century, indeed, destitution had been considered a punishment, not a sign of election. People were inclined to view it as the price to be paid for sin, and, at the social level, as an affliction as inevitable as illness, which could hardly be cured. Wealth, on the contrary, was regarded as a token of divine favor. It afforded the opportunity of acquiring merit by making donations to churches and by handing out alms to the poor. Far from being a curse, it was a means of access to sanctity, provided one made good use of it by practising generosity. This last was one of the basic values of the knightly ethic. The most fervent were offered the possibility of giving up their riches. But such renunciation implied prior ownership. As for the poor, they were under the obligation of praying for their benefactors, whose souls would thus more surely escape the pains of hell or purgatory.

Under the influence of the ideal of apostolic life, and later of the evangelical movements, an about-face occurred in this area in the twelfth century. The religious, as we have seen, found themselves confronted with the problem of wealth, as well as with problems raised by the existence of a growing number of paupers. The world of lay people did not escape this challenge. Made sensitive to it by preachers who spoke to them of Christ's poverty, many became more heedful of the destitution of the wretched and of failings in charity. The result was an extraordinary flowering of hospitals and charitable foundations throughout the West. Some gave birth to genuine religious congregations such as the Antonites, or Hospitallers of Saint Anthony, a society founded in Dauphiné in 1095 by a gentleman and his son in thanksgiving for the healing of the latter, who had been stricken with ergotic poisoning. The Hospitallers of Saint Lazarus, who cared for lepers, appeared in Jerusalem around 1120; the Hospitallers of the Holy Ghost (or Brothers of the Dove), established in Montpellier about 1180, opened hospitals in many cities throughout the West. Other lay confraternities, such as the Bridge Brothers, settled along pilgrimage routes in order to build bridges and keep them in good repair, and to provide shelter for travellers.

Finally, the Trinitarians, instituted by Saint John of Matha in 1198, sought to free prisoners and to ransom christian slaves in moslem lands. But besides these religious orders on the scale of christendom, many isolated foundations—homes for the elderly ('maisons-Dieu'), hospices or mere refuges—sprang up for the purpose of assisting the sick, pilgrims and travellers. In areas such as Lombardy or Anjou where a quantitative study has been attempted for the twelfth century, the results are impressive: all classes of propertied society—lords, both lay and ecclesiastical, burghers, parish communities and confraternities—then became actively involved in works of mercy.

Gestures of charity did not simply become more frequent. They were also carried out in a different spirit. Over time, almsgiving had become a ritual act. The great abbeys periodically fed crowds of paupers who flocked to them on certain dates: the feasts of patron saints, solemnities of the liturgical cycle, the death of one of the community's monks. On these occasions, food and money were handed out. For their part, high-placed laymen—kings, dukes or earls—permanently supported a certain number of appointed poor—usually twelve of them—who followed them in their travels. These prebendaries, who benefited from the prince's favor, had an essentially symbolic role: they allowed their patron to fulfill his obligations to the weak and the oppressed. In practise, they instead shielded their benefactor, with whom they communicated only through his chaplain, from the world of the destitute. In the course of the twelfth century, both under the influence of the social changes which increased the number of paupers and of the evangelical ideal, this ritualistic concept of charity gave way to a will to combat poverty effectively and especially to come into direct contact with the poor. The very notion of 'neighbor' underwent a development: those who must be aided included not only widows and orphans, but also the victims of injustice and all those who lived on the fringes of affluent society: the sick, lepers, prostitutes, wanderers of all kinds. Genuine charity consisted in tracking down neediness and in relieving it through an organization as efficient as the conditions of the period allowed.[32] Thus, when a severe famine struck Champagne in 1143, Count Theobald, a friend of the Cistercians and a disciple of Saint Bernard, was not content with generously opening his granaries to the deprived and with sacrificing a golden vessel which he had broken and sold as a sign of penance. He also asked that the poor who lay abandoned in the public squares be reported to him, and sent out religious to scour the towns for sick persons and lepers. All such behavior had its source in a feeling of compassion for suffering in its various forms; traces can be discerned even in the crusades of the late twelfth century. Once the eschatological and messianic prospects which had marked the first expeditions had faded into the distance, brotherly charity became the principal motivation for departure to the Holy Land. One took the cross primarily in order to free captives, defend pilgrims, and save the Christians of the East from being trampled. The increased sense of solidarity with far-off brothers immersed in misfortune aroused in many of the faithful the desire to provide assistance, financial on the part of some, military on that of others.

Under the influence of such altruistic concerns, the spirit of charity underwent a transformation. Fasting, which had long been practised in a spirit of penance, became more closely linked with charity. From the twelfth century onward, Christians rediscovered the fact that the food and possessions they deprived themselves of were pleasing to God only if given to others. But especially, the very notion of almsgiving underwent a change: growing numbers of clerics, including canonists, presented it in their writings and sermons as a duty

---

[32]On all these new aspects of charity, both theoretical and practical, during the twelfth century, see the important book published under the direction of Michel Mollat, *Études sur l'histoire de la pauvreté au Moyen Age* (Paris, 1974) 855 pp. It includes the findings of a broad collective investigation on the scale of the West.

of justice rather than as a praiseworthy act or a gesture of purification. Almsgiving was a strict obligation for the rich; alms were a right for the poor, who were entitled to claim what was due them, or even to steal it if necessary, that is, if it were refused them. Saint Bernard harshly said as much to the prelates of his time, making himself the spokesman of the destitute: 'Our livelihood goes to make up your superfluity. Whatever is added to your vanity is stolen from our needs.' Medieval christianity thereby revived the patristic tradition, especially that of Saint John Chrysostom, according to whom all that the rich owned in excess belonged to the poor. Moreover, the conviction prevailed that the outward gestures of charity must be accompanied by a personal commitment. In the late twelfth century, Raoul l'Ardent emphasized that the donor must put something of himself into the gift he made; failing that, his action was worthless. In this way he suggested the system of *elemosyna negotialis*, or committed alms, consisting, for instance, in bringing a pauper out of destitution by finding work for him instead of being content with handing him a coin.

In the last analysis, the source of this refinement of charity resided in the conviction that the poor, as replicas of the suffering Christ, shared to some extent in his saving role. Many late twelfth-century writings speak of 'our lords the poor' or present them as 'vicars of Christ'. For many lay people, unable to attain to meditation on the divine and kept away from communion by the fear of sacrilege, a renewed practice of charity provided an opportunity to meet God present in others, and especially in the most deprived. This was what young Francis of Assisi experienced on the threshold of the thirteenth century, as he himself recounted in his Testament: 'When I was still in sin, the sight of lepers seemed most bitter to me; but the Lord led me among them and I was merciful to them.' When he kissed the leper, he was in exact line with the twelfth-century evangelical movement, and may be regarded as its fulfillment.

The place held by charity in the spiritual life of twelfth-century Christians is evidenced by the existence, during that period, of many lay saints whose main virtue it was. Most of them were never canonized, but in their day they enjoyed great prestige among their fellow-citizens. Here we will mention only two particularly typical figures: the first, Saint Raymond Gayrard (d.1118), a convert of Robert of Arbrissel, was the benefactor of the poor in Toulouse, and founded a hospice for them. After his wife's death, he took over the direction of the fabric of Saint-Sernin and undertook the construction of a toll-free bridge over a river at a place it was often impossible to cross because of high water. Perhaps he must be credited with building another bridge over the Durance as well. He also seems to have been very appreciated as a popular preacher, 'obedient to church rectors, ardently burning to gather souls to God, a most virulent opponent of heretics', according to his biographer.[33] His namesake, Saint Raymond of Piacenza in Lombardy (about 1140-1200), devoted himself to the practice of charity after having spent a good part of his life on pilgrimage, especially in the Holy Land, thus earning himself the nickname of 'Palmerio'. After 1178, with his bishop's agreement, he outfitted a hospice in his native city in order to give shelter to pilgrims, to the sick, and to the poor. He soon became the defender of the last-named against unjust judges and against the rich, leading processions in which the deprived of every kind cried: 'Come to our aid, cruel Christians, for we die of hunger while you live in plenty'.[34] For him as for many of his contemporaries, the practice of works of mercy offered a spiritual agenda and a means of sanctification.

[33]Quoted by E. Delaruelle, 'L'idéal de pauvreté à Toulouse au XIIe siècle', in *Vaudois languedociens et pauvres catholiques*, Cahiers de Fanjeaux, 2 (Toulouse, 1967) p.74.
[34]Life of Saint Raymond Palmerio, in AA SS, Iulii, VI: 645–657.

THE LAITY IN RELIGIOUS LIFE

In the course of the twelfth century many lay persons, aware that their state did not *a priori* exclude them from religious life, searched for forms of life which would allow them to reconcile the requirements of an existence dedicated to the service of God with those imposed on them by their state as Christians living in the world.

Most of these experiences were inspired by ideals formulated in clerical circles. Thus in Germany, during the last years of the eleventh century, peasants embarked on the practice of the apostolic life (*vita apostolica*) after the fashion of monks and canons. According to the chronicler Bernold of Konstanz,

> In those days the common life blossomed in many parts of the germanic kingdom, not only among clerics and monks..., but even among layfolk, who with great devotion offered themselves and their possessions in order to take part in this common life. In outward appearance, they looked neither like clerics nor like monks, and yet it seems that they were in no way inferior to them in merit.[35]

Entire families and villages settled in the shadow of monasteries, particularly at Hirsau, a benedictine abbey in the Black Forest which was defending the cause of reform throughout southern Germany. In these movements, the distinction between states of life (monks, clerics, lay people) was not abolished, but it took second place, the focus being on community life in the service of Christ.

For the first time, lay people were claiming the possibility of attaining the apostolic life while remaining in their state. They included both single and married persons. All sanctified themselves by relinquishing what they owned to the clerics, following the example of the early Christians who laid their possessions at the feet of the apostles. They remained outside the abbeys, while being closely associated with the religious at

[35]Bernold of Konstanz, *Chronicon*, PL 148:1406–1407.

the level of liturgical life. At Hirsau, they were called 'extern brothers' (*fratres exteriores*). When one of them died, food was distributed to the poor for ten days, as was done upon the death of a monk. This quasi-monastic life without religious profession was not unrelated to the practice of dedication (*deditio*) whereby some individuals, out of piety or necessity, gave themselves and their lands to a monastery. They thus became ecclesiastical serfs, sometimes called saintsmen (sainteurs) because they dedicated themselves to the patron saint of the abbey or collegiate church, or *cerecensuales*. It should also be paralleled with the confraternities which associated generous layfolk with the cluniac monks, who mentioned them in their prayers. The novelty of the 'conversion' movement we have just described lies in its collective nature—we are no longer dealing with individuals but with whole lineages—and especially in its association of lay people, who offered their work, with monks whose prayers benefited the entire community—all on an equal footing. Such a movement may be connected with many early twelfth-century religious foundations in which clerics and lay persons coexisted. This was the case, in particular, in the order of Grandmont, where laybrothers were more numerous than clerics and exercised a factual ascendancy over them, or again at L'Artige and at Obazine in Limousin, where, at least in the beginning, priests and laymen led a semi-eremitic life in common.

We are, however, dealing with avant-garde movements whose impact must not be exaggerated. The will to appropriate the spiritual riches of monasticism does constitute one of the basic aspirations of the faithful in the twelfth century. But the coexistence of lay persons and clerics within the same religious community was an institutional paradox which could not survive in the radical form it had assumed at Hirsau or Grandmont. After some time, most of these groups were forced to adopt the Rule of Saint Benedict or that of Saint Augustine. Laymen still had their place, but they became, so to speak, second-class religious, that is, laybrothers. We come across them in Italy as early as the eleventh century, at Vallombrosa and Camaldoli. They proliferated throughout the West in the course of the twelfth century, and all the new orders—Carthusians, Cistercians, Premonstratensians— numbered them in their ranks. Some have chosen to see in this occurrence the end-point of a long ascent towards religious life of the elite of the monastic household *(familia)*. This seems rather improbable, since they made their appearance, not in monasteries of the traditional sort, which had many servants, but in the new ones, which had few. In actual fact, reformed monasticism, insofar as it wished to shut itself off totally from the world, could not do without auxiliaries who would ensure the community's economic survival. The existence of *conversi*, or laybrothers, who took over most of the material tasks, allowed the monks to devote themselves more freely to the specific obligations of their state. On their part, many laymen, especially in the country, longed to benefit from the temporal and spiritual protection of a religious community. For want of an education, they could not become choir monks. They thus became laybrothers (*conversi*), a term which acquired a precise institutional meaning around the years 1120-1130, to refer to religious in charge of agricultural work. They lived inside the monasteries, but their dormitories and refectories were separate from the monks'. They took no part in the liturgical services, which they attended only on Sundays and feast days, and were simply obligated to recite a few Our Fathers. In actual fact, their active collaboration in the life of the community and in their own sanctification took place through work.

The laybrothers' spirituality is ambiguous and has been the object of contradictory appraisals. As they were recruited especially among illiterate peasants, they were often regarded as inferiors by the choir monks, who had a twofold advantage over them: they were clerics and contemplatives. Thus the laybrothers often clashed with their living companions, going as far as violent rebellion in some cases. Inside the monastic institution, the sociocultural cleavages which divided secular society thus crop up again—not surprisingly. On the whole,

however, and despite its imperfections, the laybrother institution enabled many laymen access to an original form of
religious life, based on community life and work. Some of
them became saints, for instance Blessed Simon, caretaker
of the granary of Coulmis on the lands of the cistercian abbey
of Aulne in Hainaut, who was favored with exceptional graces
and in particular with the gift of reading people's hearts.
His reputation was soon so great that Pope Innocent III
summoned him to the Fourth Lateran Council in 1215 in
order to benefit from his advice.

Still another form of religious life was available to laymen,
mainly to those stemming from the aristocracy: the military
orders, which appeared in connection with the crusades. In
1118, a few knights who found themselves in the Holy Land
banded together in order to escort pilgrims and protect them.
First known as 'Poor knights of Christ', they formed a kind of
third order associated with the canons of the Holy Sepulchre.
A few years later, the Hospitallers of Saint John of Jerusalem,
who had been caring for the sick and giving shelter to the
destitute since the middle of the eleventh century, became
specialized in military tasks. In both cases, we are dealing
originally with groups of pious laymen who commuted the
temporary crusade vow into a permanent commitment to the
service of the Church. But they were not slow in feeling
the influence of monasticism and in turning into religious
orders. The first, who took the name of Templars, adopted a
rule drawn up on the model of Saint Benedict's in 1128, at
Saint Bernard's instigation. In 1130, the illustrious abbot of
Clairvaux commended these knight-monks in an important
treatise, signicantly entitled *In Praise of the New Knighthood*
(*De laude novae militiae*); in it he defined, in vibrant terms,
a spiritual ideal based on the practice of the common life, on
obedience, and on contempt for the world.

All the religious groups and orders we have just cited have
in common their attempt to achieve a synthesis between specific aspects of the lay state (work, warfare, charity) and ideals
which had until then been lived solely in cloisters (common
life, obedience, asceticism). But the weight of tradition and

the rigidity of canonical rules usually resulted in these foundations' lay character quickly fading away, as their monastic aspect became more marked. For this reason, most of the faithful who yearned for perfection did not follow such paths, but chose those of penitential spirituality, which they found more accessible. This was no absolute novelty. Since ancient times, there had been penitents in the Church, that is, lay men and women who led austere and devout lives in their own homes after receiving the sacrament of penance, which for a long time had not been repeatable. In the Middle Ages, especially beginning in the late twelfth century, an important change took place: the penitential state became a form of religious life freely chosen by those who longed for perfection, without being able or willing to leave the world. It did, however, imply a break with secular life, and was manifested for all to see by the wearing of a one-piece grey woolen habit, uniform in color. Moreover, penitents were forbidden to attend entertainments and to participate in social life. They usually refused to bear arms and to swear oaths, on account of the Gospel maxim: 'Say "yes" if you mean yes'. Those who were married made periodic continence a rule; this explains the name *continentes* which they were commonly given. These observances were a sign of spiritual transformation. They expressed medieval man's deep need to evidence conversion of heart through visible gestures.

At the crossroads of asceticism, which exerted great fascination on the faithful, and of the apostolic ideal, the penitential state joined the spirit of poverty and charity with the search for physical suffering. Those who practised it yearned to reproduce the mystery of Christ, both victim and saviour, humiliated and triumphant, in their daily existence. There was no Resurrection without a Passion. Deeply convinced of the truth of that statement, voluntary penitents mortified themselves in order somehow to compel the power of God to display itself in them.

This new style of christian life was particularly successful among women, many of whom could not be admitted in monasteries for economic or social reasons. As early as the last decades of the twelfth century, in areas corresponding to present-day Belgium, we witness the appearance of groups of women called beguines who lived in community under the leadership of one of their members without taking religious vows strictly speaking, and who combined manual work and aid to the sick with an intense prayer life. In these pietistic groups, which had their male counterparts—the beghards— and which were to proliferate throughout a good part of christendom in the thirteenth century, meditation on Christ's sufferings led to a life of penance and to a yearning for total renunciation. The priest Lambert 'li Beges', a native of Liège (d.1177), with whom the movement originated, describes their spirituality as follows: 'They listened to the word of God most avidly and put it into practice by participating with compassion in the immolation of the body and blood of Our Lord. It then seemed to them that the God of the universe was suffering his painful Passion once more, as witnessed by their many moans and their outpourings of love and devotion.'[36] They soon numbered saints in their ranks: one Juette of Huy relinquished her possessions in 1180, at the age of twenty-three, in order to dedicate the rest of her life to the care of lepers. Mary of Oignies especially well known thanks to her biographer, Cardinal James of Vitry, sums up in her person the full wealth of the beguinal current: born at Nivelles in 1178, married at fourteen, she retreated with her husband to a small leper-house where she served the sick for fifteen years after relinquishing all her property. In 1207 she came to settle as a beguine-recluse in the priory of Oignies-sur-Sambre where she gave free rein to her love of poverty, begging from door to door so as to be able thus to 'follow, naked, the naked Christ'. In her eyes, living the life of the destitute and begging for one's bread was, in the same way as

[36]Text quoted by A. Mens, 'L'Ombrie italienne et l'Ombrie brabançonne', *Etudes franciscaines* 17, Supplément (1968) 18.

sacramental communion, a means of encountering Christ and
of being united with him by following his example. With her,
charitable action found its natural continuation in an authentic
mysticism.

On the threshold of the thirteenth century, the spiritual
emancipation of the laity, which had been achieved by way
of the penitential state, was an accomplished fact. Despite
the reservations and sometimes the opposition of many clerics, we witness, around the year 1200, a mushrooming of
groups of religious laymen (*laici religiosi*) and of religious
women (*mulieres religiosae*) who strove to live their christian
vocation in the world. The canonists eventually took formal
notice of this development, as is evidenced by the definition
of the word 'religious' given in 1253 by one of their most
renowned representatives, Henry of Susa, cardinal of Ostia:
'In a broad sense, those persons are called religious who live
in a saintly and religious manner in their homes, not because
they submit to a specific rule, but on account of their life,
which is harder and simpler than that of other lay people who
live in a purely worldly fashion.'[37] There is no better way of
saying that religious life is not a state but a lifestyle.

At the cost of conflicts and condemnations which sometimes led them to the brink of heresy, the popular religious
movements of the twelfth century succeeded in making the
Church accept the main elements of a spirituality which,
though it was lived rather than formulated, nonetheless assumed considerable importance in the history of medieval
christianity. Historians have been inclined to neglect it because it remained implicit. Without this new climate, neither
the content nor the success of the franciscan message could be
accounted for. One of the great lessons which emerged from
the experiences lived by lay persons in the twelfth century was
the possibility of living the Gospel among men while rejecting

[37]Henry of Susa (Hostiensis), *Summa aurea*, book III (Venice, 1570)
193.

the 'world'.[38] And such was the goal set for the brotherhood of the Penitents of Assisi by the son of the merchant Bernardone. We shall not detract from his originality by emphasizing that he was tributary to the spiritual currents that had stirred christendom a few decades earlier. His contemporaries made no mistake in seeing in the Friars Minor the successors the Waldenses and in the Friars Preachers those of the regular canons. It is to Saint Francis' immense credit that he achieved a synthesis, at the highest level, of the sometimes contradictory aspirations of the previous generations. Devotion to the Christ of the Gospel venerated in his humanity, his cross and his Passion, went hand in hand in him with an acute sense of God's omnipotence; a longing for purification and humility was coupled with total faithfulness to the Church and with a basically optimistic view of the created universe which made him insensitive to the temptations of dualism. In him, an apostolic thrust and a sense of asceticism, love of poverty and a spirit of obedience, were united in an exceptional way. We have had to insist here on aspects of his sanctity which appear as end-points. But we must not forget that his life was among those events which, though not inexplicable, nonetheless upset the normal course of history.

[38]The term must be understook here as referring to creation vitiated by sin.

IV

MEDIEVAL MAN IN SEARCH OF GOD

The Forms and Content of Religious Experience

IN THE MIDDLE AGES even more than in other periods, the longing to live an intense spiritual life was inseparable from adopting a form of religious life, usually defined by a rule endowed with sanctifying value in itself. This was not incompatible with the search for more immediate and intimate contact with God. Here we should speak of prayer. We must admit quite clearly that, aside from the liturgical prayer of monks, we know almost nothing about it. Epic poems—the *chansons de geste*—have preserved some fine prayer texts, but are we dealing with literary developments or with habitual expressions of personal piety? The Our Father and the first part of the Hail Mary were doubtless known to everyone. The psalms seem to have been in favor among clerics as well as among cultured layfolk, who very soon had them translated into the vernacular for their use. But we must resign ourselves to not knowing how often and in what spirit they were recited. Here we are faced with a gap which the historian can scarcely remedy for the period we are dealing with, but which he must not seek to conceal.

For want of being able to grasp man's relationship with God in prayer, we can attempt to trace it through other forms of piety and devotion. Unable as he was to think in the abstract and often so much as to conceive of it, the twelfth-century Christian lived his religious experience primarily at the level of gestures and rituals which put him into contact with the supernatural world. Thus his immense appetite for the divine sought satisfaction in overt acts bearing a strong emotional charge, while their theological content often remained quite tenuous. Among these, pilgrimage undoubtedly took first place in the piety of the faithful. Taking up the pilgrim's staff meant, primarily, travelling to a sacred space where the divine power had chosen to show itself through miracles. Such privileged spots were many, and they proliferated in the West during the twelfth century. Next to regional shrines such as Rocamadour or Sainte-Foy at Conques, the faithful increasingly went on far-off places of pilgrimage such as Santiago de Compostella, Saint Michael of Gargano, or Saint Nicholas of Bari. Rome also became a frequent goal, not to mention Jerusalem—for the crusades did not interfere with trips to the Holy Land any more than did the capture of the city by the Turks in 1187. Aside from this last case, the well-attended places of pilgrimage were those possessing precious relics. These were the object of intense veneration on the part of both clergy and faithful, as evidenced by the splendor of the shrines and reliquaries in which they were locked. As living and palpable signs of God's presence, their main function was the performance of miracles.

Miracles played a large part in the spiritual life of the time, and this is not true only of the laity. Along with visions, they were one of the most important means of communication between this world and the next. The idea that God went on revealing himself to men through wonders was present to every mind. Thus medieval Christians were constantly in search of miracles and were ready to acknowledge them in any extraordinary occurrence. Those who performed them were regarded as saints. The Church rejoiced at numbering a great many of them within her ranks: at a time when heresy was shaking its structures, were they not tangible proof that

God was still with her? As for the ordinary faithful, the miracles they expected from God's servants were primarily cures: restoring peace of mind to the possessed, making the lame walk and the blind see were the main criteria of sanctity in those days. Until a regular procedure for canonizations was established at the end of the twelfth century, miracle-working power remained practically the sole condition required for a deceased person to enjoy the honors of a cult. Sanctity was verified by its effectiveness. Since physical evil, like sin, was the work of the devil, miraculous cures could come only from God and sufficed to prove that he or she through whose intercession they had been obtained belonged to the heavenly court.

The desire for direct contact with the divine also expressed itself in eucharistic devotion. Except for penance, Mass was the only sacrament that counted during the medieval period. But the faithful attended it less to receive Christ's body than to see it. Against the spiritualist heresies and especially against catharism, the Church during the twelfth century stressed the real presence of God in the Eucharist, 'true body and true blood of Christ'. This emphasis on the down-to-earth aspect of the sacrament found a deep echo in the religiosity of the people, who attended Mass as a spectacle, awaiting God's descent to the altar. Thus the faithful, longing to gaze on what was hidden in the sacrament, pressured the clerics into showing them the host at the very moment the divine mystery took place. This was the origin of the rite of elevation, which was regulated at the beginning of the thirteenth century to correct frequent abuses: in some places, priests were forced to display the host three times during Mass; in others, the moment of consecration was drawn out unduly. Indeed, it was commonly believed that looking at the consecrated host had salutary effects. For many people, it replaced sacramental communion, since the latter was rarely possible precisely on account of the veneration surrounding the sacred species. All of this points to a notion of the sacred which may be found in many religions: God, at this level, appears as an entity exterior to man. He is totally other, a mysterious and anonymous power bearing little relation to the God of the Bible. Even specifically christian rites, such as the consecration of the host, underwent the influence of this religiosity, strongly permeated with magical thinking. We could logically conclude from this survey of popular devotions that we are squarely in the field of superstition and that the practices we have just described have nothing to do with the history of spirituality. However, a number of signs indicate to the careful observer that piety was developing, if not in the direction of spiritualization, at least in that of a more pronounced christian character. Admittedly, when they went on pilgrimage, the faithful of the twelfth century, like those of carolingian times, repaired to a place where God acted through relics and then always strove to pass under the saints' reliquaries in order to obtain the desired cure. But the meaning of pilgrimage was itself evolving. In the twelfth century, pilgrims traveled more readily to the shrines of the apostles and to places where relics of Mary or of Christ, or objects which had been in contact with them, were venerated. It is easy to wax ironical about the incredible trophies the crusaders brought back from the East, as well as about the numberless teeth of Saint John the Baptist or hairs of Christ which churches in the West obtained from skillful impostors, often for high prices. The unbelievable naïvete of the faithful and the clerics' self-interested blindness should not, however, lead us to forget that the success of such devotions was, so to speak, the small change of evangelism. At the level of the masses, this expressed itself as 'an obviously clumsy and fantasizing longing to meet Christ in his mortal life' and as 'an effort to make contact with the concrete living conditions of the Holy Family'.[1] The development of the pilgrimage at Rocamadour is very instructive in this regard. At the

[1]E. Delaruelle, 'La spiritualité du pèlerinage de Rocamadour au Moyen Age', *Bulletin de la Société des Etudes...du Lot* (1966) 71.

beginning of the twelfth century, it was still one of many local shrines, where pilgrims from the area around Tulle came to receive chains which, after having touched the relics of Saint Amadour (Amator), were said to perform miraculous cures. During the latter half of the century a legend appeared, related by the chronicler Robert of Torigny, according to which this Amadour had been none other than a servant of Mary, who had helped her bring up the boy Jesus. The story is, of course, pure fabrication. But the fact that the clerics of Rocamadour induced the faithful to model themselves on someone who had lived very familiarly with Christ and his mother and who had received the vocation of serving them is not devoid of interest. The same legend emphasized that Amadour was a poor man, moreover, and praised him for his humility, all of which is very much in line with the spirituality of the time. This is no isolated example. It does seem that in the twelfth century the faithful's attention turned to the great names of the early centuries of the Church, whereas the early Middle Ages had witnessed a proliferation of saints devoid of serious testimonials who were merely expected to perform cures, without there being any thought of taking them as models or even of being moved by their lives.

Moroever, during this period penitential spirituality began to enrich rites which belonged to paganism rather than to the christian faith. Indeed, we witness the spread of a conviction that human efforts accomplished on behalf of God or of his saints somehow compelled the divine power to reveal itself. In the eyes of the faithful, leaving their familiar surroundings for quite a long time and braving the dangers of travel were meritorious actions which must find their reward in miracle. We may consider such a notion of the relations between man and the divine to be still very prosaic; it was nonetheless an improvement inasmuch as it established a connection between the grace expected of God and the Christian's personal effort.

Finally, the very idea people had of sanctity did not remain static. Before the twelfth century, hagiography presents us with saints who appear mysteriously predestined to their state.

The faithfulness with which they observe the divine law is less a result of an ascent toward spiritual perfection than the perceptible expression of their having been chosen by God. In the treatises of Honorius of Autun, that spokesman of the common mentality, 'saints are born, not made'.[2] In the course of the following decades, a change took place in the way saints' lives were written. Under the influence of the new spirituality, hagiographers strove to show, sometimes rather awkwardly, that miraculous power was subordinated to an ascetic existence as well as to the practice of charity. Innocent III even stated on several occasions that miracles were valid only when guaranteed by a holy life and certified by genuine witnesses. For the first time in the history of the medieval West, the Church itself underlined the ambiguity of the signs of the sacred. Doubtless, much time was still to elapse before the requirements as to discernment defined by the papacy took on in the area of the cult of the saints. But the primacy of faith and works over the miraculous in the evalution of sanctity is one of several signs of the spiritualization that was beginning to take place within Christianity.

ART AND SPIRITUALITY

The Church was indeed striving to lift a coarse and poorly educated people beyond purely material demands by leading it to sense the existence of a higher reality. To this end, it did not hesitate to use the resources of art, both as the expression of an intense spiritual life—that of the clerics— and as a means of giving the laity a glimpse of the greatness and infinite wealth of the divine mystery. We will not study here the difficult problem of the religious formation, or rather permeation, which the faithful received through cycles of frescos or liturgical singing, or through the sculptured groups which proliferated, from the late eleventh century onward,

---

[2]Y. Lefèvre, *L'Elucidarium et les lucidaires* (Paris: 1954) 338.

on the porches of abbeys and cathedrals. A great deal has been said about the 'stone Bible' which these works offered to the gaze of simple folk. It is not certain that educational intentions were paramount in the minds of those who had them produced; they seem rather to have been aimed at making an emotional impact liable to extend into spiritual insight. In a religion in which worship remained the essential act, the main function of God's house was to offer the divine mysteries a setting worthy of their greatness. But beauty in form was not appropriate only to the sacred nature of liturgical services. The stone church, a symbol of the Church itself, of the redeemed people, was to give the faithful a foretaste of the beauty of heaven. Suger, the great abbot of Saint-Denis (1080-1151), is one of the few clerics of the time who defined with precision the religious aims which inspired the building and decoration of places of worship. In his autobiography, he developed a symbolism of light strongly influenced by the mystical theology of Pseudo-Dionysius the areopagite. According to dionysian doctrine, every creature receives and transmits divine illumination according to its capacity, and beings as well as things are ordered in a hierarchy according to their degree of participation in the divine essence. The human soul, enveloped in the opaqueness of matter, longs to return to God. It can succeed in doing so only through visible things which, at succeeding levels of the hierarchy, reflect His light better and better. Through created reality, the mind can thus rise again to the uncreated. In the field of art, such a concept of the relationship between the human and the divine led to the proliferation inside churches of objects made of silver and gold or adorned with precious stones, which, because of their radiance, could be regarded as symbols of the virtues and help man rise to the splendor of the Creator. Likewise, the light filtering through stained glass windows supported the flights of meditation and led the mind back to God, whose reflection it was. To quote the inscription which Suger had engraved on the bronze door of Saint-Denis: 'By means of perceptible beauty, the numbed soul rises to true Beauty and, from the place where it lay engulfed, it rises again to heaven when it sees the light of these splendors.'

Renewed monasticism declared war on these aesthetics—which were also those of Cluny—in the name of a rigoristic spirituality. Though Saint Bernard allowed rich decorations in churches designed for the faithful, he was opposed to them in abbatial churches and, generally speaking, among religious. Thus the statutes of Cîteaux, like those of the Carthusians, forbid placing gold crucifixes or silk hangings in conventual churches and adorning them with sculptures and stained glass windows. 'Let us leave painted images to simple folk', wrote the regular canon Hugh of Fouilloy. In Saint Bernard's opinion, all this luxury was not only useless but dangerous. First of all, the concern for a rich setting prevented clerics from giving alms to the poor. More especially, by cultivating the arts in a disorderly fashion, man ran the risk of coming to love pleasure for its own sake and of multiplying superfluous stimulations for the purpose of pure enjoyment. Did wealth and abundance of ornament not lead, in the last instance, to a search for sensual delight, with the mind dissipating itself in outer sensations and letting itself be distracted by shimmering impressions? In the eyes of the abbot of Clairvaux, all this contradicted the requirements of the spiritual life. For the soul needed inner concentration so as to be able to know itself and become unified in humility; introspection conflicted with empty curiosity, which threatened the religious spirit. But let us make no mistake! Saint Bernard and the supporters of ascetic rigorism were not enemies of art, and in a cistercian nave purity of line and simplicity of form amply make up for lack of ornament. But the irrationality and rich exuberance of romanesque art contrasted with an aesthetics of poverty which chose to restrict itself to what was necessary and retained only simple, functional shapes. Cistercian art is austere, disciplined, and based on a search for purity. It is no less steeped in spirituality than that of Cluny. But whereas, in the latter the joyful abundance and wealth of forms aimed at dazzling the mind and giving it a foretaste of everlasting festivities, the new art saw an obstacle to contemplation in such material realities. For the supporters of asceticism and voluntary poverty, only through bareness could man attain spiritual love, which made vital necessities into a springboard toward God. Thus not one but two spiritualities of art existed during the medieval period: one accepted and even sought the mediation of perceptible things; the other rejected the analogy between the beauty of the world and the splendor of the Beyond. For supporters of the latter, the ascent toward God implied humility and renunciation of the carnal use of the senses. The role of art was then restricted to favoring man's return to his inmost self, which awakened him to the inner life.

A CONQUEST: THE INNER LIFE

As piety underwent a process of individualization and religion became more personal, the life of the spirit ceased to be the privilege of monks. In a society which was beginning to free itself from outward constraints and to curb blind violence, a growing number of clerics and lay persons acquired that minimum amount of leisure and distance from instinct which makes meditation and reflection possible: 'Inside western man a new pioneer front opened up, that of conscience.'[3] It is certainly not by chance that this new awareness—in the full meaning of the term[4]—coincided with a certain lapse in eschatological prospects. While the masses untiringly persisted in pursuing the millenium and transferred their hopes, which had been disappointed by the mediocre result of the crusades, to successive messiahs, the best minds rediscovered the truth of the Gospel maxim: 'The kingdom of God is within you'. A change took place at the level of religious mentalities: the last judgment still figured among the essential concerns of the faithful, but it lost its character of harrowing

[3]Le Goff, 'Métier et profession', (Chapter III, note 29) p. 52.
[4]The French term *conscience*, here translated by 'awareness,' also refers to conscience in the moral and religious sense. (Translator's note)

imminence. It would soon be regarded only as 'the distant
sanction of the judgment of one's conscience in inner dialogue
with Christ'.[5]

Such a development resulted in enhancing yet more the
importance of the sacrament of penance in christian life and
in modifying its form. The essential stage of the penitential process shifted from atonement to confession. Until the
eleventh century, indeed, sin was not deemed to have been
remitted until the penalty inflicted for it had been entirely
accomplished. From the twelfth century onward, the generally accepted notion was that confession was the essential
gesture and that absolution was an accomplished fact as soon
as confession had been made, for the Church acknowledged
that it was such a humiliating and difficult act that in itself
it possessed expiatory value. It is therefore not surprising
that from then on the sacrament of penance was referred
to as 'confession'. The mind's turning back toward itself, its
becoming conscious of its misdeed and of the offence given
God were henceforth more important than the increasingly
easy actions which penitents continued to carry out by way of
satisfaction. More generally speaking, the twelfth century was
marked in the spiritual sphere by an attitude which has been
called 'christian socratism'. Men of such different tempera-
ments as Abelard, Saint Bernard, and Hugh of Saint Victor
shared the conviction that in order to know heaven and earth
it was first of all necessary to know oneself. *A fortiori*, the
soul would be able to reach God only after a lengthy journey
through the meanderings of the human psyche and the steps
of the intellect: 'How do you ask to see me in my brightness,
you who do not know yourself?' says God to the soul in
a bernardine work. Far from being a detour, introspection
henceforth appeared as a necessity for anyone aspiring to live
at a level higher than that of instinct.

[5]M.-D. Chenu, 'La fin des temps dans la spiritualité médiévale', *Lumière
et Vie* 11 (1953) 101-116.

According to monastic tradition, the privileged meeting place between the individual conscience and God was Scripture. For in the Middle Ages the Bible was not one book among many others, but *the* book which held the key to all mysteries. People learned to read in it, and attempted to discover in it the laws ruling the life of human beings and of the universe. God was almost physically present in it: solemn oaths were sworn on the Bible, and one would open it at random in order to read in it one's destiny or seek one's vocation. Saint Francis did so at the moment of his conversion. Such a book was not intended to be read. In fact, even among monks, few indeed possessed the entire text, and its content was far from invariable. Important differences were to be found from one copy to the next, and the notion of canonical scriptures meant almost nothing during a period when apocryphal texts such as the gospel of Saint Peter and apocalyptic treatises were readily incorporated into the Bible. The knowledge which both clerics and laity had of it was nearly always an indirect one. The texts most often quoted were those which occurred in the liturgy: the psalms, the synoptic Gospels, the letters of Saint Paul and the Book of Revelation. As a result, the faithful were well acquainted with some books, and virtually ignorant of others. Every believer drew from this vast heritage according to his abilities and his needs. The literature relating to the crusades afforded ample room to the Old Testament, with its tales of the wars waged by the people of God and its descriptions of the Holy Land, and also to the Book of Revelation which nourished the eschatological hopes of the masses. Under normal circumstances, most of the faithful were more interested in the psalms and in the Book of Job, which abounded in moral precepts and down-to-earth maxims. The clerics in city schools were fond of speculating on Genesis, which brought out God's action as creator, and contemplatives, beginning with Saint Bernard and William of Saint Thierry, took pleasure in commenting on the Song of Songs interpreted as a chronicle of the tumultuous wedding of God and the human soul.

For medieval man, therefore, the Bible was a reality with which he was more or less deeply permeated, but which, in all cases, nourished his spiritual life by providing him both with matter for reflection and with directions for action. Reminiscences and quotations crowd the writings of clerics in such large numbers that it is often difficult to make out what proceeded from their own minds and what belongs to the sacred text. The latter was both interiorized and updated, so much so that it became part of personal experience. For Scripture was not regarded as a mere narrative of salvation history. Beyond its obvious historical meaning, a subtle exegesis, which sometimes tended to drift towards allegory, discovered an appropriate moral and spiritual significance in every episode, if not in every word. This manner of approaching the biblical texts entailed the risk of dissolving facts in a very rich but not always coherent symbolism. How tempting it was to seek answers to each and every question in a book whose author was God himself!

During the first decades of the twelfth century, the urban schools developed a method allowing access to an understanding of the divine mystery while avoiding what might have been vague and subjective about the traditional biblical commentaries. With Abelard, theology—since that is what we are dealing with—became an autonomous discipline, resorting to logical reasoning and dialectics. God remained the object of knowledge, but one sought to attain him through natural reasoning, not through outpourings of the heart. Scripture was not excluded from the field of reflection, but was placed on the same level as pagan authors, particularly Plato and Aristotle, whom the West was beginning to rediscover. In some intellectual circles—especially parisian ones—the idea prevailed that the principal truths of Christianity, including the mystery of the Trinity, could be accounted for by using the concepts and methods of pagan philosophy. Saint Bernard was disturbed by this and accused Abelard and his disciples of bringing revealed truth down to the level of human truth. It is not our intention to relate the long and painful controversy which pitted the abbot of Clairvaux against the 'knight of dialectics', whom he blamed for trusting the aptitudes of reason too much. What matters for our purpose is that with Abelard theology broke away from the 'sacred page' (*sacra pagina*), that is, from the spiritual commentary of the Word of God. From then on, we must deal on one hand with a scholastic theology which was a rational speculation on revelation, and on the other with a mystical one which remained centered on the meditation of Scripture and refused to favor intellectual reflection as a means of access to the knowledge of God.

THE ORIGINS OF WESTERN MYSTICISM

There was another deep divergence between the theological and the mystical way: the latter's objective was not to wrest God's secrets from him, but to allow the soul to experience his presence and to be united with him. The biblical text, which, for the spiritually-minded, remained the necessary reference of all religious experience, provided a starting point for meditation, which led by stages to contemplation. Many twelfth-century authors, from Aelred of Rievaulx to Saint Hildegard, have described this passage from reflection to enlightenment from personal experience. According to them, the divine Word first acts upon the mind like a flame, severing the bonds which join it to the flesh and to sin. Once the memory has been purified, the soul can use the words and images of the text as a foothold in its attempt to rise toward its Creator. At the end of a series of ascending stages, it crosses, as by means of a ladder, the infinite distance separating it from God. Confessions of unworthiness are gradually replaced by surges of affection. Finally, in silence, the Word takes possession of the soul and becomes flesh: man gives birth to God. As Saint Bernard says: 'The Word's speech is the infusion of his gift' (*Locutio Verbi, infusi doni*). The Word who speaks to human persons and who gives himself to each of them are one and the same. The spirit emerges elated and dazzled from these uplifting moments. Thanks to Scripture, man can free himself from his own limitations, since in it the visible and the invisible meet.

With Saint Bernard and William of Saint Thierry—both of them Cistercians—, such mystical experiences, always present in a diffuse way within monasticism, were carried to their farthest consequences and presented in systematic fashion for the first time. Both of them took as a starting point the Song of Songs, an especially lyrical book of the Old Testament which was interpreted as a dialogue between God, identified with the lover, and the soul, presented as the Almighty's beloved. Starting from there, Saint Bernard developed in a grandiose vision a whole dialectic of the relationship between the Creator and his creatures. According to him, man is in the image of the world through his body, in that of God through his soul. On account of original sin, the divine element in man has been overshadowed by evil. But God has restored this likeness through the Incarnation: Mary, the new Eve, is not only the instrument of the new creation, but a model for Christians of all times. The soul-bride in search of God must strive to resemble the Virgin and, like her, to become a mother in order to give birth to the divine spirit. From that moment on, man rises above his fleshly and sinful condition and finds his way back to the heavenly home for which he yearns from the bottom of his heart. The abbot of Clairvaux distinguishes four steps in this ascent: carnal love, which consists in loving oneself, then love of neighbor and of Christ's humanity which is already higher, although still on a mediocre level. If the Christian perseveres, he will come to love God in his sweetness and to obtain spiritual consolations. But God will not come down into the soul until she has become capable of loving him for himself, after having completely shed her carnal husk. Once she has reached this stage, the soul-bride, like the Church whose figure she is, lives according to love. In her all the potentialities which go to make up human nature become supernaturally actualized. Far from being an abnormal occurrence, mystical ecstasy is the soul's perfect fulfilment inasmuch as it allows God to be known inthe deepest recesses of the trinitarian mystery. Saint Bernard was too much of a realist to be unaware of how exceptional such states are, and he himself clearly underlined that the mystical experience is inferior to the face-to-face vision of God which would occur in heavenly bliss. But, as at the Transfiguration the apostles participated in Christ's radiance, the ecstasy afforded the soul by the Bridegroom's kiss conforms her to some extent to the loved one to whom she is spiritually united. Through mystical union, man does not become God, but he rises above himself and receives by grace what God is by nature. In a being thus deified, the divine image is definitively restored.

The spiritual themes found in the writings of William of Saint Thierry (d.1148), author of the *Mirror of Faith* (*Speculum fidei*) and *On Contemplating God* (*De contemplando Deo*), are more or less the same as those developed by his friend Saint Bernard, but there is more emphasis on the trinitarian mystery. The human soul, in William's eyes, is the created image of the creating Trinity—a doubtless inferior and debased image, but one nevertheless modeled on it. For, according to him, the Fall did not destroy the basic likeness, but merely clouded it. By relying on grace and on personal effort, a human being athirst for perfection may restore this likeness by reattuning his soul to the Trinity. In order to achieve this, he will have to rise from the animal to the rational state, and from the latter to the spiritual one, which lets him share in the glory of the Resurrection here below. In those who establish themselves at this level, the three faculties of the soul regain their true function—memory brings man back to the Father, reason leads him to Christ and will to the Holy Spirit—and open up onto an intimate knowledge of the triune God.

The mysticism which arose in the West in the twelfth century was not restricted to the cistercian current alone, important though it was. Indeed, other ways were experimented with in the search for union with God. Some authors strove to associate intellectual reflection with a loving quest for the divine presence. This was the case, in particular, in the School of Saint Victor, a house of regular canons founded in Paris in 1113 by William of Champeaux and made famous by a series of great theologians and spiritual teachers, chief among them Hugh (d.1141) and Richard (d.1173) of Saint Victor. The latter is the more interesting from our viewpoint, for he developed a doctrine often called 'speculative mysticism'. For Richard, the author of a treatise on the Trinity (*De Trinitate*), the Holy Trinity is the highest object of contemplation. In order to attain to knowledge of this mystery, speculation, that is, rational investigation, is the first stage. One must discover the necessary reasons which allow the intellect to grasp the foundations of trinitarian life. But, according to him, contemplation alone, founded on Scripture and nourished by love, allows access to the intimate life of the divine persons. God awakens in the human soul a haunting and unquenchable longing which drives the creature to merge with him in a leap of the mind beyond itself (*excessus mentis*) which, according to Richard, is an enlightenment rather than an ecstasy properly so called. Though the goal pursued is, as for Saint Bernard, intimate union with God, the Victorines view it primarily as a vision of the profound meaning of things and of beings. Their thought process abolished, or rather was unaware of, the barriers set up by later spirituality between the ascetic, intellectual, and mystical lives. For them, the ascent toward God implied the analysis of psychological realities, the exploration of the soul's faculties, and the steps of contemplation. This concept of the spiritual life—one both synthetic and dynamic—had scarcely any influence in its own day. But it opened the avenues on to which a Saint Bonaventure was to venture in the thirteenth century.

Other mystical experiences, most especially in feminine circles, took devotion to Christ's humanity and a longing for active participation in the Saviour's Passion as a starting point. This current is not unrelated to the cistercian school, and both Saint Bernard and William of Saint Thierry gave the mystery of the God-Man an important place in their experience and in their writings. Both had, however, emphasized that devotion to the humanity of Christ was merely one of the very first steps of love. In their view, one could go from shadow to light, from earth to heaven, only by gazing on God in his divinity, and the soul in quest of perfection had to rise from meditation on Christ according to the flesh to contemplation of Christ according to the spirit. In the religious movement which developed in the diocese of Liége and in Brabant at the end of the twelfth century, those aspects played an essential part, however, and adoration of the suffering Christ lay at the heart of the mysticism which then blossomed in cloisters and beguinages. Saint Lutgard and Mary of Oignies sought to be united with God in his incarnation and poverty. From then on, and for at least a century, the emotional element became dominant in western mysticism. Its essential components were a pathetic feeling for the drama of Redemption, meditation on the bloody sacrifice of Christ, the gift of tears which purified the inner gaze and expressed compunction of the heart. Should we see in this feminine mysticism no more than a popularized reflection of Saint Bernard's ideas on the soul's relationship with its Creator? In so doing, we would be minimizing the originality of the Low Countries' spirituality; we would also be forgetting that a half century rich in change separates the abbot of Clairvaux from the beguine recluse of Oignies. He saw the flesh as no more than a shadow and an obstacle beyond which one had to go in order to rise up to the eternal Word; for her, Christ's body, both as an instrument of salvation and as a token of eternity in its eucharistic continuation, was at the heart of the christian mystery.

All religions have witnessed and witness various degrees of participation in the mysteries they teach. Medieval Christianity is no exception to the rule: from the cult of relics to bridal mysticism, it offers a broad spectrum of ways of access to the divine. It may seem strange to lump together such different forms of religious expression. But the stress laid by theologians on the role of the incarnate Word in the Redemption and the upsurge of popular devotions to the persons of Christ and his mother express the same intuition, though doubtless at different levels. The orientations of piety have by no means been proven to be always dependent on that of the lofty spirituality lived in cloisters. In the twelfth century, the two apparently developed concomitantly, and in some features, the religion of the masses may even have been ahead of that of the elite: devotion to the Holy Lance, miraculously discovered before Antioch by the crusaders, preceded the Brabant mystics' veneration for the wound in Christ's side by several decades. Beyond these problems of influence, which are always delicate and difficult to solve, the historian notes that on the threshold of the thirteenth century two basic certainties permeated the religious consciousness of the West: God could be reached only through his crucified Son, and in order to achieve salvation, it was necessary to model oneself on Christ. But there are several ways of identifying with a loved one: seeking out his footsteps and cultivating his memory, imitating his example or attempting to be one with him. Different though these attitudes are, they are nonetheless inspired by the same feeling.

V

REFLECTIONS

A T THE END OF THIS STUDY, in which we have consistently sought to place spiritual currents within the flow of history, one question cannot fail to come up: what is the nature of the bond between the development of spirituality and the transformations which occurred in medieval society? By insisting at all costs on establishing a connection between these two orders of facts, do we not run the risk of underestimating the role of great figures— Saint Peter Damian or Saint Bernard, for instance—and of underrating the timelessness of their message? After all, even today many men and women find an answer to their expectations in monastic rules, although the present-day world is very different from the one in which the religious experience from which they sprung took place.

The personal role of a certain number of great saints in the history of spirituality cannot be disputed, but it is quite obvious that their message would have found no response had society not been in a position to receive it. It is striking to note, as L. Genicot has done, that 'spiritual demands increase as economic necessity grows less stringent'.[1] Is it by chance

---

[1] L. Genicot, 'L'érémitisme dans son contexte économique et social', in *L'eremitismo in Occidente nei secoli XIe XII* (Milan, 1965) 45–69.

that the carolingian period, characterized by low agricultural production and meagre commercial activity, was also the era of religious conformism, and that the best minds of the time considered spiritual life only from the angle of moralism? Be that as it may, beginning in the eleventh century and especially in the twelfth, when rapid economic and urban expansion became a general phenomenon in the West, the ruling climate of lifelessness gave way to a spiritual ebullience whose most visible manifestation was the proliferation of forms of religious life. Intellectual renaissance was accompanied by a renewed interest in interiority. Or rather—for such distinctions are too modern—the widening of the slim fringe of those who, in western society, gained access to the life of the mind brought about both cultural progress and a rise in the level of religious aspirations.

We can follow this development in a precise manner by considering the attitude of religious orders toward property. Eleventh and twelfth-century monastic reformers accepted and even sought donations of land which allowed them to increase their abbeys' possessions. Later on, the supporters of the apostolic life—especially the Cistercians and the regular canons belonging to the new observance (*ordo novus*)—simply wished to have enough land to meet their needs and refused the benefit of land rents to avoid being trapped in the seigniorial system. Stephen of Muret advised the Grandmontines to have so little land that it would not free them from the necessity of begging. Finally, in the thirteenth century, Saint Francis forbade his brethren to own anything, either indivdually or in common, and enjoined them to provide for their living by work or, if that failed, by begging. This gradual detachment from all forms of property and power was made possible by the deep transformations undergone by western society between the tenth and the thirteenth centuries. To allow a religious group to free itself from the manorial system and rule out the ownership of reserves, in kind or in money, there had to be enough cities, work openings, and charitable burghers. The failure of some premature experiments in rejecting property is significant in this regard. Thus Odo of Tournai who, at the end of the eleventh century, attempted to have a community of regular canons live by the work of their hands was forced, following a plague, to fall back into line and to adopt the Cluniacs' way of life.

The example we have just studied is not entirely convincing, inasmuch as the economic system of religious orders is only a consequence—and when all is said and done a secondary one—of their spiritual choices. The same cannot be said of poverty, which held a central place in a good number of religious movements during the medieval period. And the extolling of poverty in western spirituality coincides strikingly with the general rise in living standards. During the carolingian era, it did not benefit from any favorable bias: destitution could hardly be regarded as a value in a society of want. From the twelfth century onward, on the contrary, there were enough rich people to allow it to be held up as an ideal. In the thirteenth century, in the urban, trading world of central Italy, it even appeared as *the* evangelical virtue, and Saint Francis, in whose eyes evil was identified with the false security and the power of oppression provided by money, gave a choice place to 'Holy Poverty' which 'confounds greed and avarice and the cares of this world'.[2]

Conditioned to some extent by the economic framework in which it is inserted, spiritual life is likewise dependent on social relationships.[3] The role of the abbot and the notion of obedience are not at all identical in the benedictine rule and in the mendicant orders. More deeply still, representations of God were influenced by the structures of feudal society. Medieval man conceived his relationship with his Creator on the model of that existing between a king and his vassals.

[2] *Salutatio virtutum* (11), in *Ecrits*, ed. K. Esser, SCh 285 (1981) 272.
[3] As has been aptly shown by Barbara H. Rosenwein and Lester K. Little in their article, 'Social Meaning in the Monastic and Mendicant Spiritualities', *Past and Present* 63 (1974) 4–32.

The latter were personally and indissolubly bound to him by the bonds of homage. Likewise, a Christian could not deny his God without felony, since through baptism he had renounced Satan in order to follow Him. He was thus under the obligation of restoring His rights when they were infringed on by heretics or infidels. Could a good vassal see his lord dispossessed without reacting? There, surely, we have one of the mainsprings of the crusading spirit, at least at the level of the military aristocracy.

Does this amount to saying that the inflections in spirituality which we have noted between the eighth and twelfth centuries were mere adjustments to the transformations undergone by western society during that time? In fact, things are far from being so simple. First of all, the success of a new form of religious life adapted to the changes which had taken place in the secular world rarely brought about the demise of those that had existed previously. The rapid development of the regular canons in the twelfth century did not weaken the monastic institution, any more than the success of popular religious movements caused laybrother recruitment to dry up. Moreover, even when deep changes took place in the spiritual sphere, they did not merely go along with the general evolution or follow it: they sometimes provided solutions to problems at which society and the Church were balking. In most instances, the answer was not obvious. Thus in the case of poverty: even though the increase in resources gradually made it appear a possible lifestyle, its becoming a positive spiritual ideal still required a reversal of values. Acknowledging the worth of destitution, whether voluntary or not—that is, of a difficult and socially humiliating condition—, adopting it and proposing it as a path to salvation and ascent to God, as the twelfth-century evangelical movements and especially Saint Francis did, meant both finding an answer to the problem of evil, which the Cathars were holding up as a rival to God, and allowing a world in which social distances and tensions were becoming more pronounced to emerge from its own contradictions.

Next to these variations of the religious ideal—which, following the example of economic historians, we might call conjunctural—, we come up against long-term movements in the history of medieval spirituality. Their existence becomes obvious as soon as we step back a little from data and doctrines. The most important of these general tendencies is the one leading to a growing personalization of religious life. During the early Middle Ages and even during the feudal era, the faithful could not contemplate coming into contact with the supernatural except by means of gestures which gave them a hold on it, so to speak. This was the time when the liturgy played a basic role for both monks and layfolk, even though the latter hardly understood its meaning. What was crucial in their eyes was scrupulous observance of the rituals, which were mysteriously effective in themselves. Thus epic poems (*chansons de geste*) frequently depict knights giving one another communion as *viaticum* in the form of a flower, a blade of grass, or a little earth, when there was no priest to distribute the sacraments.[4] It is as though the reception of the Saviour's body mattered less than the rite of eating. In such a religious universe, human freedom played only a limited role. Whether a man was saved or damned was not up to him; evil could swoop down on him without warning and make him its prey, without his responsibility being directly involved. The devil's presence in him would be displayed by vices with respect to which he would be less a culprit than a victim. The soul was at stake in a struggle beyond its control; it was a battleground rather than an active force.

Starting in the twelfth century, the attitude of western man toward his spiritual destiny began to change. No longer resigned to being the plaything of obscure forces, he undertook

---

[4]Thus in *Raoul de Cambrai*, ed. Le Glay, p. 95, Raoul gives his companions the Eucharist in the form of grass: 'to many a gentleman he gave communion with three shoots of grass, since there was no priest' ('mains gentix hom s'i acumenia de trois pous d'erbe, qu'autre prestre n'i a').

to react against them. For some, both clerics and lay persons, this fighting will took the form of radical spiritualism: in order to triumph over evil, they sought purity and salvation in the rejection of the flesh and of matter. Many of them also challenged the Church's visible aspects (hierarchy, sacraments, tithes, and other things), expecting forgiveness solely from the intercession of men who made evangelical perfection a reality in their lives. Other currents, which remained within the bounds of orthodoxy, strove to give meaning to human effort and suffering by relating them to the pains and torments endured by Christ. They gave rise both to penitential spirituality and to a religion based on good works which met with brisk success in the world of the laity and from which the crusades, the ascetic movements, and the 'revolution of charity', all of which we have studied earlier, sprang. In this new spiritual climate, freedom, and especially the Christian's personal responsibility, were much greater. He was able to take an active part in his own salvation and to win heaven, so to speak, by the sweat of his brow. In particular, he could prepare for the final judgment by resorting to the sacrament of penance and by encountering Christ in the poor. Finally, in a limited elite, the personalization of spiritual life blossomed into an act of union with God based on mystical experience, whose starting point became the devotion to Christ's humanity. The soul, moved by consideration of God's love for his creatures, then succeeded in contemplating—if only for a moment—his intimate mystery, then to enjoy many consolations in return.

The refinement and interiorization of the spiritual sense go hand in hand during the medieval period, as we may note in connection with the forms taken by conversion. In the early feudal age, a Christian who experienced a conversion was duty bound to flee the world, either by shutting himself up in a cloister or by going off to the desert. The break with a sinful existence was manifested primarily by the rejection of temporal society and of secular life. In the twelfth century, these outward forms of conversion certainly existed and even became commonplaces of hagiographic literature: a saint who had not followed such a spiritual journey could scarcely be imagined. But the word *conversus* took on a new meaning: it referred either to lay persons who had put themselves under the protection of religious and had offered them their work, or to the growing numbers of men and women who put themselves at the service of the poor in hospices and leper-houses. Soon, with the Penitents, conversion was brought down to the practice of a rule involving the rejection of the purely worldly aspects of secular existence, but lived in human society, with no change of state. Once this process reached its end-point, flight from the world had been completely interiorized.

We would not wish to bring this book to a close without pointing out to the reader how temporary and incomplete a synthesis we have just presented. In setting it forth, we have been led to emphasize known facts and established findings. In fairness, we should also have brought out the important gaps which exist in our knowledge of medieval spirituality and the problems which remain unsolved, usually because they have not been correctly formulated. We will give only one example: popular spirituality. According to the all-too-rare evidence available, it appears to be a deep and coherent reality which, from time to time, rose to the surface of history, and whose main components are the extolling of the lowly, a penitential spirit, and the will to appropriate the spiritual riches of monasticism. This set of beliefs and aspirations came to light in collective outbursts of fervor which, from translations of relics to the crusades, periodically interrupted the usual lifelessness of the masses' religious life. It remains to be explained how this spirituality formed and what its relationship was to that of the clerics.[5] We shall not regret ending on a confession of ignorance, provided the latter may stimulate research in a field which has great need of it.

[5]Interesting elements on the subject may be found in *Les religions populaires*, edd. B. Lacroix and P. Boglioni (Québec, 1972) 50–74.

TABLE OF ABBREVIATIONS

PL   J.P. Migne, *Patrologia Latina . . . series Latina*. Paris. 1844–1866.

RB   *Regula monachorum Benedicti The Rule of Saint Benedict*

SCh Sources chrétiennes. Paris. 1941–.

BIBLIOGRAPHY

GENERAL WORKS

Brooke, Rosalind B. and Christopher, *Popular Religion in the Middle Ages. Western Europe 1000–1300* London: Thams and Hudson, 1984.

Leclercq, Jean, François Vandenbroucke, Louis Bouyer, *The Spirituality of the Middle Ages,* A History of Christian Spirituality, 2. London-New York-Paris: Desclée, 1963 [Paris: Aubier, 1961].

Histoire spirituelle de la France. Paris: Beauchesne, 1964 (pp.43-124).

Genicot, Léopold. *Aux sources de la spiritualité occidentale.* Paris: Cerf, 1964.

Morghen, Raffaello. *Medioevo Cristiano.* Bari: Laterza, 1958.

Southern, R.W. *Western Society and the Church in the Middle Ages.* London: Penguin, 1970.

Vauchez, André. *The Laity in the Middle Ages. Religious Practices and Experiences.* Notre Dame, 1992.

Violante, Cinzio. *Studi sulla Cristianità medioevale.* Milan: Vita et Pensiero, 1972.

I. THE GENESIS OF MEDIEVAL SPIRITUALITY

Frantzen, Allen J. *The Literature of Penance in Anglo-Saxon England.* New Brunswick, New Jersey: Rutgers University Press, 1983.

Heitz, Carol. *Recherches sur les rapports entre architecture et liturgie à l'époque carolingienne.* Paris: S.E.V.P.E.N., 1963.

Jungmann, J.A. *Missarum sollemnia. Eine genetische Erklärung der römischen Messe.* 2 vol. Vienna 1948, 5th edition, 1962. French translation: *Missarum sollemnia. Explication génétique de la messe romaine,* 2 vol. Paris: Aubier, 1950. English translation: *The Mass of the Roman Rite.* New York, 1950.

Riché, Pierre. *Daily Life in the World of Charlemagne.* Philadelphia: University of Pennsylvania Press, 1978 [*La vie quotidienne dans l'Empire carolingien.* Paris: Hachette, 1973].

Vogel, Cyrille. *Le pécheur et la pénitence au Moyen Age.* Paris: Cerf, 1969.

II. THE MONASTIC AND FEUDAL AGE: The Late Tenth and Eleventh Centuries

Brooke, Christopher. *The Monastic World 1000-1300.* London: Paul Elek, 1974. Also published as *Monasteries of the World.* New York: Crescent, 1982.

Bultot, Robert. *Christianisme et valeurs humaines. La doctrine du mépris du monde en Occident de saint Ambroise à Innocent III.* Paris: Naewelaerts, 1963, 1964.

Chiesa e Riforma nella spiritualità del secolo XI. Todi, 1968.

Cohn, Norman. *The Pursuit of the Millenium.* London: Secker and Warburg - Fairlawn, NJ: Essential Books, 1957.

Duby, Georges. *Adolescence de la chrétienté 988-1140.* Paris: Skira, 1967.

———. *L'an mil.* Paris: Julliard, 1967.

Gougaud, L. *Dévotions et pratiques ascétiques du Moyen Age.* Paris, 1925.

Lawrence, C.H. *Medieval Monasticism. Forms of Religious Life in Western Europe in the Middle Ages.* New York: Longmans, 1984.

Miccoli, Giovanni. *Chriesa gregoriana.* Florence: La Nuova Italia, 1966.

Milis, Ludo. *Angelic Monks and Earthly Men. Monasticism and its Meaning to Medieval Society.* Woodbridge, Suffolk - Rochester, New York: Boydell, 1992.

Pacaut, Marcel. *Les ordres monastiques et religieux au Moyen Age.* Paris: F. Nathan, 1970.

Penco, Giorgio. *Storia del monachesimo in Italia dalle origini alla fine del Medio Evo.* Rome: Paoline, 1961.

Southern, R. W. *Saint Anselm. Portrait in a Landscape.* Cambridge: University Press, 1990.

Il Monachesimo e la riforma ecclesiastica (1049-1122). Milan: Vita e Pensiero, 1971.

Spiritualità cluniacense. Todi, 1960.

III. THE RELIGION OF A NEW ERA: From the Late Tenth to the Early Thirteenth Century

Alphandéry, Paul and Alphonse Dupront. *La chrétienté et l'idée de croisade,* 2 vols. Paris: A. Michel, 1954, 1959.

Cathares en Languedoc, Cahiers de Fanjeaux, 3. Toulouse: Privat, 1968.

Chenu, M.D. *La théologie au XIIᵉ siècle.* Paris: Vrin, 1957. Translated by Jerome Taylor and Lester K. Little, *Nature, Man, and Society in the Twelfth Century.* Chicago-London: University of Chicago Press, 1968.

Coole, P. *The Preaching of the Crusades to the Holy Land (1095-1270).* Cambridge, Massachusetts, Harvard University Press, 1991.

Delaruelle, Etienne. *L'idée de croisade au Moyen Age.* Turin: Bottega d'Erasmo, 1981.

Grundmann, H. *Religiöse Bewegungen im Mittelalter,* 2nd edition. Hildesheim, 1961.

Leclercq, Jean. *Bernard of Clairvaux and the Cistercian Spirit.* Translated by Claire Lavoie. Kalamazoo: Cistercian Publications, 1976. [Paris, 1966]

Le Goff, Jacques. *Hérésies et sociétés dans l'Europe préindustrielle, XIᵉ - XVIIIᵉ siècle.* Paris: Mouton, 1968.

Little, Lester K. *Religious Poverty and the Profit Economy in Medieval Europe.* Ithaca - London: Cornell University Press, 1978.

Manselli, Raoul. *L'eresia del Male.* Naples: Morano, 1963.

Manteuffel, Tadeusz. *Naissance d'une hérésie. Les adeptes de la pauvreté volontaire au Moyen Age.* Paris: Mouton, 1970.

McGuire, Brian P. *The Difficult Saint. Saint Bernard of Clairvaux and His Tradition.* Kalamazoo; Cisterican Publications, 1991.

Meersseman, Giles Gérard. *Ordo fraternitatis. Confraternite e pietà dei laici nel Medio Evo,* 3 vol. Rome: Herder, 1977.

Mollat, Michel. *Recherches sur les pauvres et la pauvreté dans l'Occident médiéval,* 2 vol. Paris: Sorbonne, 1974.

Nichols, John A., and Lilian Thomas Shank ocso, edd. *Peace Weavers.* Medieval Religious Women, 2. Kalamazoo: Cistercian Publications, 1987.

O'Callaghan, Joseph F. *The Spanish Military Order of Calatrava and its Affiliates.* London: Variorum, 1975.

Petit, François. *La spiritualité des Prémontrés aux XIIᵉ et XIIIᵉ siècles.* Paris: Vrin, 1945.

Povertà e Ricchezza nella spiritaulità dei secoli XI e XII. Todi, 1969.

Power, Eileen. *Medieval English Nunneries.* New York-London: Biblio and Tannen, 1964.

Richard, Jean. *L'esprit de la croisade.* Paris: Cerf, 1969. Berkeley: University of California Press, 1959.

Shank, Lilian Thomas ocso and John A. Nichols, edd. *Distant Echoes.* Medieval Religious Women, 1. Kalamazoo: Cistercian Publications, 1984.

Tierney, Brian. *Medieval Poor Law. A Sketch of Canonical Theory and its Application in England.* Berkeley: University of California Press, 1959.

Vaudois languedociens et Pauvres catholiques, Cahiers de Fanjeaux, 2. Toulouse: Privat, 1962.

IV. MEDIEVAL MAN IN SEARCH OF GOD: The Forms and Content of Religious Experience

Beer, Frances. *Women and Mystical Experience in the Middle Ages.* Woodbridge, Suffolk - Rochester, New York: Boydell, 1992.

Blumenfeld-Kosinski, Renate and Timea Szell, edd. *Images of Sainthood in Medieval Europe.* Ithaca-London: Cornell University Press, 1991.

Bynum, Caroline Walker. *Jesus as Mother. Studies in the Spirituality of the High Middle Ages.* Berkeley: University of California Press, 1984.

Chenu, M.D. *L'éveil de la conscience dans la civilisation médiévale.*Montreal-Paris: Vrin, 1969.

Delaruelle, Etienne. *La piété populaire au Moyen Age.* Turin: Bottega d'Erasmo, 1975.

*Il dolore e la morte nella spiritualità dei secoli XII e XIII.*Todi, 1967.

Duby, Georges. *L'Europe des cathédrales, 1140-1280.* Paris: Skira, 1966.

Gilson, Étienne. *Saint Bernard: un itinéraire du retour à Dieu.* Paris: Cerf, 1964.

Le Glay, Marcel. *Li romans de Raoul de Cambrai et de Bernier.* Geneva: Skatkine Reprints, 1969.

McDonnell, Ernest W. *The Beguines and Beghards in Medieval Culture, with special emphais on the Belgian scene.* New Brunswick, New Jersey: Rutgers University Pres, 1954.

Pellegrinaggi e culto dei santi in Europa fino alla prima crociata. Todi, 1963.

Rubin, Mizi. *Corpus Christi: The Eucharist in Late Medieval Culture.* Cambridge: Cambridge University Press, 1991.

Sargent-Baur, Barbara N., ed. *Journeys towards God. Pilgrimages and Crusades .* Kalamazoo: Medieval Institute Publications, 1992.

Ward, Benedicta, SLG. *Miracles and the Medieval Mind. Theory, Record and Event, 1000-1215*. Philadelphia: University of Pennsylvania Press, 1987.

INDEX

CISTERCIAN PUBLICATIONS
Texts and Studies in the Monastic Tradition

TEXTS IN ENGLISH TRANSLATION:
- Monastic insights from the desert, and from christian monks and nuns East and West
- Cistercian homilies and treatises from the formative twelfth and thirteenth centuries

STUDIES OF THE MONASTIC TRADITION:
- Its history, customs, architecture, liturgy, and influence, from desert beginnings through the Middle Ages and into the present day
- Reflections on prayer and the christian vocation by contemporary contemplatives
- Audio and video resources on monasticism as well as books published abroad and not readily available in North America

All books are available singly or by series standing order. Standing order customers automatically receive new titles as they appear at a 25% discount from the list price

SERIES:
- CISTERCIAN FATHERS
- MONASTIC WISDOM
- CISTERCIAN STUDIES
- CISTERCIAN LITURGY

EDITORIAL OFFICES
Cistercian Publications • WMU Station
1903 West Michigan Avenue • Kalamazoo, MI 49008-5415   USA
tel 269 387 8920   fax 269 387 8390
e-mail cistpub@wmich.edu

CUSTOMER SERVICE—NORTH AMERICA: USA AND CANADA
Cistercian Publications at Liturgical Press
Saint John's Abbey • Collegeville, MN 56321-7500 USA
tel 800 436 8431   fax 320 363 3299
e-mail sales@litpress.org

CUSTOMER SERVICE—EUROPE: UK, IRELAND, AND EUROPE
Cistercian Publications at Columba Book Service
55A Spruce Avenue • Stillorgan Industrial Park
Blackrock, Co. Dublin, Ireland
tel 353 1 294 2560   fax 353 1 294 2564
e-mail sales@columba.ie

To explore the range of titles offered by Cistercian Publications, please request our free complete catalogue from one of the customer service offices or visit our website at **www.cistercianpublications.org**